DEDICATION

...to the 350 million year old order Odonata, *elegant
and primordial nobility of the slime.*

Flyfishing Still Waters

By Donald V. Roberts

Fly drawings by Loren Smith

All other illustrations by Donald V. Roberts

Photographs by Diana Roberts

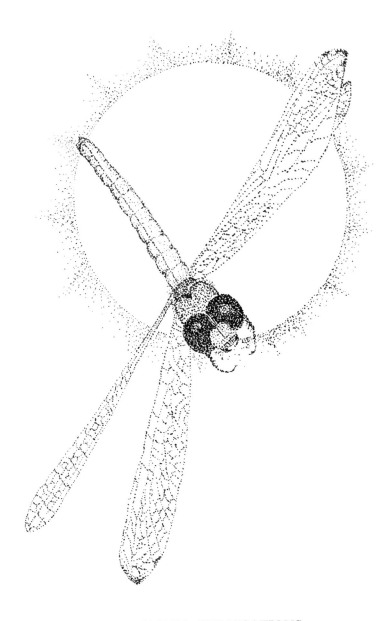

FRANK AMATO PUBLICATIONS

P.O. Box 02112, Portland, Oregon 97202

ABOUT THE AUTHOR

On a July day in 1956, Donald Roberts loitered by a gray backwater in an Oklahoma gully and watched two amber dragonflies mate in mid-air. A year later a Pawnee Indian woman, shrunken and fragile with age, read of the intrusion in the lines around his eyes.

The thought of naiad counsels remained with him as he crossed the plains on a one-way journey west. The shadow of the mountains held his spirit cool and fast. He never returned to the flat lands. He bartered for his eventual education on "The Hill" (Washington State University) by farming, driving a truck, mopping floors, trafficking food on a tray in a fancy beanery, and tutoring juvenile delinquents. He once worked for a total of one day in an aluminum factory. "It smelled and felt like the earth was boiling below me."

Water, moving and still, and its inhabitants continued to perplex him. Fly fishing developed into ceremony, and writing became the payment of homage.

Today, Donald Roberts lives in John Day, Oregon (the result of a detour somewhere outside of Colfax, Washington) with his blond wife, Diana, beside whom the golden trout pales, and two children, whose infant incivilities encouraged much of the research for this book. He is an art teacher by trade, but an angler by inclination. "The distinction between vocation and avocation is beginning to blur."

Mr. Roberts is currently contributing to the fly fishing renaissance in his capacity as editor of the magazine, *Flyfishing the West.* He describes the birth of each issue as a ritual in natural evolvement.

Much of his writing, indeed most of his thinking, is explained in a naturalistic sense. "I am inspired by the dragonflies and their slender cousins, the damselflies, which never cease to crisscross my soul, like lake bottom ooze, with a multitude of tracks."

Contents:

Introduction 6

I.   An Angry Birth 7

II. Lakes: Scratching the Surface 8

III. Equipment: Poles Apart 15

IV. Trout: Depth Perception 19

V.   Flyfishing: Nymph O'Mania 22

VI. Nymphs: Adolescents of the Deep 29

VII. Profiles: A Line on Lakes 49

VIII. Conservation: Barbed Arguments, Barbless Hooks . . 67

IX. Landing Without a Net: A Future Parable 72

Photo by Pat Trotter

Introduction

ost fishermen would like nothing better than to get to know, befriend, maybe move in with a river or stream. To cavort with a flowing beauty is akin to fantasies of conquest involving buxom Hollywood starlets. Unfortunately, a vague platonic longing is as close as most of us ever get to either. Aside from the all too occasional forays, the quickies to the distant rivers, where we discover that the stonefly hatch ended yesterday, most of us are not allowed anything resembling a consummate relationship with moving water.

The modern fisherman, an unwilling pawn of technology, must of necessity become resigned to the less obvious passions of lakes and reservoirs. Lakes are, at least, abundant.

One old river fisherman, a strict breed, asked me once, with pity aplenty, "How do you love a reservoir?"

He took me by surprise, and I had no glib response, no witticism, not a single insight to offer. I had never given it much thought and was taken aback with my own lack of understanding. I finally muttered something about "availability"...better an ugly girl than no girl at all.

I am indebted to the old river fisherman for making me think, for adding emotional dimension to my still water longings. If he asked me the same question today I would answer with the confidence of a passion much rehearsed.

"Rivers are so obvious in their beauty that they inspire infatuation. Lakes require study, commitment. Rivers flow only one way. Lakes have infinite patterns, moods, guises. Rivers are brash and constant in their conversation. Lakes are quiet, haunting, lyrical."

Despite the fact that each lake and every reservoir is an enclosure, an impoundment, a land-locked container, it is also a mini-universe as infinite as the vastness of outer space.

The irony about my obsession with lakes is that what I cannot see fascinates me the most. I recall one particular occasion in an art gallery. Robert Sterling, a professional artist of repute in the Northwest, was standing before a large abstract painting. He was literally locked into the ambiguous and amorphous space suggested by the canvas. After several minutes of reflection, I turned to him and asked, "What is it about this painting that you like?"

Sterling smiled slightly and replied, "It's what you can't see..."

The pulse of life which frequents the inner spaces of lakes provides a constant source of inquisitive irritation. It is impossible for an eclectic to pass up such temptation. After all, fly fishing by its very nature is a contemplative endeavor. But even at its most leisurely pace it is active rather than passive, and never are the rewards entirely contingent upon landing fish. The discovery of an unusual species of insect can be as volatile a natural experience as hooking a Methuselahan trout. The natural gratuities, which accrue with every quest for fish, transform every fishing excursion, even the most fishless, into an ecological odyssey.

Nymph fishing, especially with a sinking line, is the most introspective form of the hallowed art. It requires discipline and faith, but most of all, a fertile imagination. As one stands with his feet grafted to the bank, or his posterior stoically embalmed upon a wet boat seat, with the high-density line threaded into the dark material of a lake, one is compelled to conjure up images of a subterranean netherworld. The nymph must be presented as an aggressive sacrifice. It must be jerked headlong across an underworld landscape, through jungles and over sparse plains, before the wary eyes of aquatic predators.

Nymph fishing is the strongest proof that fishing without the mind would be a barren art.

When "...the long light shakes across the lakes..." (Tennyson) you would have a difficult, no—impossible, time convincing me that my affair with lakes is not justified adultery.

Chapter I

An Angry Birth

In the time when the mountains still steamed from the womb and only rivers dampened the earth, there roamed a gigantic, silver-maned grizzly. This irascible old bear, a creature as ancient as rounded granite, delighted in his vast territorial reign.

During one of his many autumn odysseys down the sunset side of the Cascades, he felt a hunger as wide and as empty as the sky. He stopped at a coastal river too young to have a name and with one paw scooped out all of the fish. He engorged lustily on the squirming meal. Feeling heavy and drowsy, Grizzly settled back on a grassy bank in the sun and slumbered while his long, black, splendid tail languished, cooling in the river current.

Meanwhile, the barnacle-encrusted grandmother of all Brown Trout returned from feeding at sea to discover that entire generations of her offspring had disappeared. Brown Trout peered up through the river froth and swam into the shadow of the fat bear. She measured the magnificent tail dangling in the river and lunged forward with her serrated jaws spread wide for slashing. Brown Trout chopped off the gorgeous tail where it joined Grizzly's broad hindquarters. Grizzly awoke with a bawl that made entire groves of aspen quake forever.

Grizzly regarded his pruned backside, first with disbelief, then with awful, mounting rage as his reason for vanity sank into an emerald pool. Brown Trout fled for her life as the sympathetic river roared with laughter. Grizzly followed, swiping and biting at the sinuous river which aided Brown Trout's wild flight. Finally, in clumsy, homicidal desperation and to prevent Brown Trout from ever going to sea again, he ripped the river loose from the earth and tied it into a colossal knot. The river, now tied like a tongue, never spoke again, except in sighs, and the water grew still and deep.

Grizzly, still unsatisfied with his revenge, pursued Brown Trout in the dark, tranquil water. Having nowhere to escape from the lunging bear, she leapt from river to river across the entire land. Grizzly tied knots in rivers until his paws grew numb, and upon seeing the sun blaze across a strange sea, he gave up the chase to wander back to his mountain home. Brown Trout became the meanest and most cautious of all fish to haunt the water recesses.

Today there lies a vast array of sighing lakes, shimmering like opals inset on the breastplate of the continent.

...Translated from carvings by Hygelac of the Weider-Geats upon basalt of the Columbia Escarpment, 12 A.D.

Chapter II

Lakes: Scratching the Surface

"Down and back at day dawn,
Tramp from lake to lake,
Washing brain and heart clean
Every step we take."

Charles Kingsley

akes, instead of pills, should be prescribed for modern man. Nothing can defuse the blood pressure, reduce the triglycerides, or unclog the sludge-lined arteries like a fishing excursion to a tranquil lake, especially if one has the gumption to forsake the snorting, oil and gas spewing outboard motor. More great mayfly and caddisfly hatches have been destroyed by the scumming effects of outboard motors on alpine lakes than by any other of man's myopic tamperings.

Anyone traveling by air over the Northwest will experience an enormously diverse topography sequined by countless lakes. Washington State alone has more lakes than the 10,000 boasted by Minnesota. From the vantage of an altitude of 25,000 feet our rich heritage of aquatic resources becomes glaringly evident.

In order to successfully fish one of the vast array of lakes, one must understand both the visible and invisible terrain of still waters. Each lake, reservoir, and pond has its own distinct identity, although for the sake of categories those in the Northwest may be loosely fitted into three basic groups: alpine, lowland, and high desert.

The alpine lakes are the esthetic jewels of natural history. They are myriad in size, shape and depth, a result of the turmoils in the earth. Most of the alpine lakes are a direct product of glacial scouring, the gouging and mountain sculpting effects of ice barges afloat on waves of rock.

In terms of fishing, the noteworthy features of the alpine lakes include a relatively short season of exposure (freedom from ice and snow), an explosive cycle of plant and animal life, irregular subsurface formations, and uniformly frigid water, rarely surpassing 55° F. Many alpine lakes are the almost exclusive domain of the cold-blooded brook trout.

The lowland lakes are a gentler breed. They are more temperate, support a larger variety of life (including water skiers), are more accessible, and are more generally embraced within the culture and commerce of man. The lowland lakes vary the most in size, ranging from square miles to square feet in scope. The lowland waters include lakes, reservoirs and ponds of every description. There are more than two million ponds alone scattered across the United States. Most of these ponds are relatively shallow and are conducive to heavy vegetation.

The high desert lakes are unique to the Northwest and occupy a special place in the viscera of many fishermen. A majority of these desert lakes are man-made, a result of water diversion for the sake of agriculture. Others have been formed naturally by peculiar enclosures of basalt in water catchment areas and spring fed depressions.

The ecology of the desert reservoirs is often unusual, even bizarre. The entire aspect of the setting is generally forbidding, hostile, and alien. The shoreline, the floral edging, and large surrounding area is a meld of primitive elements. There is little transition between land and water, but simply an overlapping of barren features. Loneliness and desolation are the dominant features of a desert reservoir. But appearances are deceptive.

There is no place more conducive to the rapid growth of fish than in the highly alkaline, seemingly sterile waters of desert reservoirs.

A vast knowledge about the type and character of lakes is esoteric but useless, unless this knowledge can be related to the activities of fish. Fortunately, general and practical principles regarding the habits and activities of trout can be somewhat uniformly applied to all types and kinds of still water. However, no single principle can supersede the employment of skilled observation. The fisherman who takes note of every unique feature and of every nuance of each lake's ecology has predisposed himself to a uniform rate of success.

Luck is not a factor worthy of anything more than tolerant disdain and fleeting recognizance. At best luck is merely included in the meaningless phrases of passing fishermen.

A simple "How are you doing?" is more encouraging and definitely less infuriating than the vacuous "Having any luck?" The latter question suggests that if you caught fish, it had little to do with your fishing prowess, and if you did not catch fish, it implies that you have been black-balled by fate, or that your very appearance

A windswept lowland lake. Notice the effects of clearcutting. There are several natural trout "lies" along the reeds and man-made structures.

is offensive to the mystical overlord of nature. Such an unflattering, bush-league question is usually answered by me with an unintelligible, if not less than friendly, grunt and threatening shake of the flyrod.

Fish Regions

The first and perhaps largest obstacle to catching trout is locating them. Fish, like all other animals, reside in the neighborhood of food and cover. However, lake fish are much less territorial and much more mobile than their river brethern. The huge inverted environ of a lake offers trout more places *not* to be than places to be at any given moment. Still, there are some reliable methods of locating trout.

Water temperature is a basic clue to the location of trout. Most species of trout prefer water temperatures in the range of 50° to 65° F. Brook trout are a notable exception, becoming quite active in temperatures as low as 40° F. Lake water in the ideal temperature range is oxygen saturated, a condition which encourages trout movement, promotes the growth of aquatic vegetation, and induces the development of insect life.

All but the most shallow lakes are stratified structures. For the sake of simplicity it is best to think of lakes as being composed of four separate strata of varying depths: The meniscus, the epilimnion, the thermocline, and the hypolimnium. Each layer is flexible, expanding and contracting in response to the changing temperatures.

The meniscus, surface film, is the micro-thin skin of the lake, which is actually a misnomer because there is no real membrane of any kind. Surface film is actually the tension created by the conflict of the air pressing against water, the resistance of lake to sky. Surface film is a floor for some miniscule, delicate insects and a ceiling for others. For many nymphs the surface film can be a barrier that must be penetrated or a kind of preserver which suspends the creature, buoys it on the surface.

10

In some instances surface tension can be great enough to provide a death trap for midges and tiny crustaceans. While surface tension is an obstacle for some insects, it is the necessary stepping stone to adulthood for others. The larval form of mayflies, mosquitoes and some damselflies spend a brief, but highly dangerous period locked by their body hairs in a kind of surface film limbo. If they survive the predations of euphoric trout, their wings unfurl, and they flit skyward toward the brief sexual encounters demanded of the species.

The epilimnion, top layer, of a lake is usually a depth comprising about one-fourth of the total cross section area. Almost without exception the top layer is the most expansive horizontal layer because of its conformity to the irregularities of the rim of the container. The epilimnion encompasses every arm, inlet, bay and shoreline distortion of the most abstract or organically shaped lake.

The top layer has the great advantage and blessing of containing the food shelf, that highly vegetated layer which extends to the edge of the precipitous innards of the lake. Trout are almost always found to be lingering on the periphery of the food shelf and sometimes in the thick of it. It is there that fish most consistently find an abundant harvest of emerging nymphs, and lurking crustaceans.

The top layer is the most susceptible to the sun. In the spring this layer heats up quickly, which stimulates fish activity. Unfortunately, the epilimnion is also the bed preferred by plankton and photoplankton, that green soup which is composed of microscopic plants and animals. Although lake bloom rarely extends below a depth of ten feet, many fishermen are discouraged and deceived by its unpalatable appearance. Fish regularly cruise that area which lies directly below the blanket of bloom.

The stubborn fisherman can overcome the bloom by fishing a sparsely dressed nymph on a sinking line. Simply allow the line to slice through the offending salad. Then give the line a couple of abrupt and energetic jerks to free the nymph of any minute debris which may be adhering to the fly. The retrieval should be a measured action which will keep the fly on a course parallel to the suspended plankton. Employment of this method will often allow the tenacious fisherman to monopolize the lake, while others stand about narrowly eyeing the split pea soup.

The middle layer, thermocline, of a lake is the most difficult layer to anticipate. While it is easy to imagine fish aggressively hunting in the many chambers and foyers of the food shelf or even lying along the silted shadows of the lake bottom, it requires special faith to devote attention to that featureless space of the broad central layer. Yet there are times, especially during the so-called dog days of August, when trout inhabit this barren layer like the fruit trapped in the jello layer of a parfait. During the harsh extremes of summer, when the sun and still air seem to promote stagnation, the termocline often becomes the most comfortable, oxygen-loaded layer. Nymphs, which must ascend through this layer, are bushwhacked like the ducks in a slowly-ascending shooting gallery.

During the intemperate, torrid season, when lowland and desert lakes are profoundly affected, the most reliable method for probing the thermocline is the cast and count approach, a kind of hunt and peck system. Using this technique the emphasis is on strength and distance rather than on precision and finesse. The longer the line cast out the better the odds on success. It takes approximately 30 feet of line simply to reach the thermocline, but much more to effectively explore the lateral area. The fisherman should "gut" cast as much line as he and his equipment

An alpine lake on a somber day . . . bad for the tourists, good for the fisherman.

can endure. Once the line hits the water, the count should begin. It has been my experience that the high density lines sink at a rate of about one foot per two seconds. Experiment by beginning your retrieve at ever-increasing depths, adding five to ten seconds of sinking time to each subsequent cast. If and when you hook a fish, take note of the number at which you began your retrieve. The odds are in favor of a repeat performance.

The hypolimnion (bottom layer) is a sanctuary from the extremes of both summer and winter. During the winter the warmer water, containing the greatest concentration of oxygen, sinks to the bottom. The fish follow it. There is never a time when trout are entirely dormant. Although frigid conditions bring a pall over their activity, trout continue to feed the year around. Prolonged hot weather can affect the metabolism of fish as profoundly as bitterly cold weather. In the summer, when the upper layers in shallow lakes become tepid, trout seek the relatively cool recesses of the bottom. In all but the deepest lakes, the floor of the lake is a kind of steady state, loosely forested terrain, inhabited by colonies of nymphs, leeches, planeriums, and thousands of other ooze-loving creatures. Large trout are often quite content to remain in the dark splendor of the lake's basement community during the major portion of their life cycle.

Because of the consistent maintenance of temperature, cover and food, the bottom layer of a lake is a territory which appeals to a constant population of fish, but not fishermen. Dragging a fly across the remote waterscape of a gothic underworld requires a tenacious spirit, a sensitive handling of equipment, and a "beyond basics" knowledge of water-borne larvae.

12

The Edge, Hedge and Ledge

Nothing about fish or fishing is totally predictable, yet there are certain factors which are basically dependable. When searching for trout, remember that fish can generally be found in one or more of the alliterative areas: the edge, the hedge and the ledge.

As on rivers, fish often lurk right at the edge of the water. The shoreline of a lake is the most neglected and foolishly approached area on the water. Too often fishermen trundle directly up to the shoreline and begin flogging the water, never aware of the trout scattering before them. The extreme edge of a lake not only provides a smorgasbord of emerging nymphs and hapless terrestrials but also the cover of large rocks, drooping willows, fallen trees, and manmade structures.

The fisherman who approaches the edge cautiously and casts skillfully is liable to catch fish in the first one or two feet of water. Other fishermen never suspect.

I have been attempting to hook one antiquated rainbow in Strawberry Lake every year for the last four years. We are now practically on a first name basis. That old fin-beast nestles at the foot of a rock in two feet of water, less than ten feet from the steep bank. His hold is perennial; he is always there, darting out occasionally to suck in a caddis larva or slog down a struggling grasshopper. He has a back as dark as midnight and a skeptic's reticence. Twenty times he has shot out from his shadowed lair, a blur which destroys my thought processes like a well aimed laser beam. But without fail this shrewd predator halts abruptly a midge-whisker away from my nymph, to regard it like an old school librarian sniffing out pornography. I don't ever expect to hook that solitary critic, and, furthermore, I'm not sure I would have it any other way.

The most conspicuous trout territory on any lake is marked by the entry of a river or stream. Not only does the moving water provide aeration, but it delivers a steady selection of nymphs, served up cafeteria style. Allowing a nymph to drift across the current and down into the still water on a sinking line can prove enormously productive, especially early in the season when caddis larvae are being washed downstream in large numbers.

The hedge refers to the profusion of weed beds found in areas along the shallows and gentle slopes of almost every lake. Aquatic vegetation creates a maze-like environment for a myriad of nymph forms, cover for trout, and a vigorous nitrogen-oxygen exchange area attractive to all water dwelling animals. These weed beds are usually characterized by dense areas of growth interspersed with irregular pockets and corridors. Trout loiter in the thick of the weed beds, facing toward the cavities like hotel occupants with windows on the central foyer. A weighted nymph fished on a long leader and a floating line can be applied with mercenary results. The devious angler will drape the line across the weed beds but will allow only the leader to broach the openings. The disturbance caused by the main body of the line will be largely obscured by the heavy weed growth. The nymph should be allowed to sink for a few seconds while all remaining reverberations die out like receding echoes. Then the rod is lifted slightly, and the nymph is activated as if it suddenly realized its vulnerability. Trout often appear suddenly behind the nymph to punctuate the properly described process like an exclamation point at the end of the line.

Picking pockets in this manner is a shallow water technique every bit as intriguing as it is productive.

Most lakes are cupped in the earth like amoeba-shaped bowls with broad, flanged rims. The ledge or drop-off which separates the open water from the food shelf is a natural holding area for fish. It is from this vantage point that fish can monitor the largest and most diverse radius of subterranean topography and still hang in the rocky or weeded confines of the precipice.

For some fishermen locating fish is largely an intuitive process; for others it is an exercise in constant study and experimentation. Becoming familiar with a variety of lake ecologies will serve greatly to demystify the intuitive process. The man who spends an inordinate amount of time on the water gradually develops a sense of perception which defies explanation. The natural extension of the senses is a reward which transcends the act of fishing.

Despite the obvious compensations of attending still waters, beware when you hear the cry of the loon. According to a Nisqually Indian legend, too much study in the laboratory of the great outdoors can transform the fisherman in ways entirely unexpected.

An Indian boy, upon seeing what a fine day it was, ignored the orders of his mother and went to the lake. He swam until he grew hungry, then fished. He finally succeeded in catching a swift trout, which he cooked and ate upon the shores of the lake. He devoured the speckled trout, unaware of the evil spirits hidden in the fish. Just as the boy swallowed the last bite, he was changed into a loon. Frightened, he flew home. Round and round he flew over the lodge, calling to his mother. The mother drove the loon away forever.

To this day the loons give harsh cries of warning to boys (fishermen?) who disobey their mothers (wives?).

An alpine lake in a symphony of light.

Chapter III

Equipment: Poles Apart

"And now I see with eye serene
The very pulse of the machine."
                    Wordsworth

ome kids touch a basketball, a baseball bat, or a football and feel something sing in their arms. Instead of leather, rubber, or wood, I touched the discolored cork grip of an old bamboo fly rod and felt a slightly dissonant chorus erupt in my bones. It's the closest I have ever come to anything truly athletic. Unlike the pool shark with his cue stick poised, I have never become obsessed with refining and sharply orchestrating the lyric qualities of my fly rod.

I have always found that an adequate manipulation of the necessary tools was all the physics needed for catching fish. I have never been intrigued by dropping flies into lawn borne hula-hoops, and I have no compulsive desire to attempt to shoot a cast across the Grand Canyon. My demands upon myself over the mastery of technique have been subordinated to the total experience of fly fishing. That decrepit old bamboo pole was merely a divining rod which pointed inexorably to the remaining enigmas of the water world.

Nevertheless, without the proper tools, that singing in your casting arm may be heard as a frustrated wail, the prelude to a fishless requiem. It is impossible to learn the craft, and surely not the art, of fly casting while trusting in the employment of inferior equipment.

The venerable Izaak Walton stated, "As no man is born an artist, so no man is born an angler."

Fly casting, like any other skill, must be learned. Learning is largely a matter of determination and practice, aided substantially by the proper tools. Although there are a lot of authoritative texts on the subject of fly casting, I would advise that the best primary instruction is accomplished through personal contact with an experienced fly fisherman.

Fly casting and fly fishing are not necessarily synonymous. The bulk of a beginner's learning experiences should occur on the water. Nothing can stimulate learning like the electric pulse of a hooked fish. On the other hand, the beginner who is not stubborn and determined will never become a fly fisherman. I know a dozen anglers who claimed without hesitation that they desired to learn to fly fish, but in actual fact they were, and still are, spinning gear junkies.

A fly rod carried along as a trunk ornament does little to assist the learning process. If you really want to learn to fly fish, you must go "cold turkey". Leave the spinning gear at home—or better yet, sell it or give it away.

There is no sense going into rhapsodies about tools, as I believe a modest accumulation of the appropriate equipment is all that is necessary. The key to acquiring the most economical and utilitarian equipment lies in the virtue of compromise. To properly nymph fish lakes one does not want a rod too short or too light to deliver a long cast. On the other hand, one does not want a rod that is too long and too heavy. The exaggerated rods deny the grace and facility which ensures pleasurable performance over the duration of a long day.

The dogma and doctrine of much fly fishing literature would lead the beginner to believe that a different setup is required for every type of fly angling. There is no denying that the collector's syndrome is a common affliction. And, of course, there are those who are more interested in the aura of the fishing culture than in actual fishing.

The bewildering assortment of graphite and cane rods on the market today is inhibiting. While cane is surely an aesthetic luxury and graphite the promised substance of miracles, the technology of neither so far exceeds the virtues of fiber glass as to make their acquisition a must. Fiber glass rods are both versatile and forgiving. A well designed glass rod will deliver the power for long casts, plus the control needed for delicate presentation. Fiber glass will also endure the abuse inflicted by the beginner as well as by the slovenly graduate. No rod, no matter how expensive, how exacting or how exotic will transform an awkward caster into a superfluid artisan.

On a comparative basis, fiber glass rods will do the same work as cane, but not with the same ease and sensual gratification, two traits which become recognizable only after years of experience. Cane is simply more biological. It whispers phrases, speaks in a soothing tone as you cast. Still, the language for all good rods is basically the same. And for most fishermen, given the costs, fiber glass is impressively articulate.

The highest objective of graphite is to accurately imitate the properties of cane. Although no graphite rod has been developed which is as sensitive and responsive as a good cane pole, power has become graphite's calling card. Graphite rods have the backbone to quickly subdue fish and to extend casting distances. An already skilled caster will obtain greater range with graphite, although not necessarily more finesse.

Despite all comparisons, a fly rod is a very personal piece of equipment. In no other sport are you as intimately "connected" at all times to the paraphernalia of the craft. Fly fishing is an unbroken continuation of man, rod and line. In final analysis, only the individual fisherman can choose how best to complete that connection of man and equipment. Many of the differences in rods are purely psychological. The brain-set of the fisherman is the final determining factor.

No matter what type of rod you choose to purchase, beware of inferior equipment. There is a glut of unadulterated garbage displayed luridly in sport shops and hardware stores across the country. Patronize a shop that specializes in fly fishing equipment and be suspicious of bargain priced gear. There is definitely a bottom-line cost for rods as well as for reels and lines. Any piece of equipment which retails below a respectable bottom-line is almost assured of being the stuff which clutters garages and fills closets for time in memoriam.

Rods

The same people who would experience coronary thrombosis at the unveiling of a

$60 price tag on a rod, would fork out $300 to $1,000 on a firearm without flinching.

"Sixty bucks for a fishin' pole!" A rolling of the eyeballs, a clutching at the sternum, a dazed, backward stumbling.

The cold, blue metals, the heft, the polished wood grain, and the oiled, moving parts of a gun give the impression of precision and complexity, seemingly in keeping with the expense incurred. Despite the absence of moving parts which click and rasp reassuringly, a good fly stick adheres to the same principles and maxims of precise and clever craftsmanship as goes into the construction of firearms. In fact, many rods are the result of more actual man hours and hand crafted care than assembly-line guns costing ten times as much money.

It is nearly impossible to get a good fly rod for under $50, and I would advise that the most versatile and enduring fiber glass rods are available in prices closer to $100. Such rods will withstand heavy use and abuse for twenty years. What other precision tool costs less than $5.00 a year to use?

For the nymph fisherman requiring power but also refinement, I would recommend a rod from 7½ feet to 9 feet long, that takes a 5 or 6 weight line. As a general rule for open water, the longer the rod the more work the rod will do. A long rod delivers long casts. The more water you cover with each cast, the less maneuvering and the fewer casts you will have to make.

Lines

There are two basic lines which I consider a necessity for nymph fishing. One is a weight forward, floating line, and the other is a weight forward, fast-sinking line. I prefer the weight forward lines because they are by far the easiest lines to blast out over long distances. The peculiar design of the weight forward lines provides a built-in magnum charge which enhances the energy of the cast. It is true that a double tapered, floating line can be coaxed to alight with more feathery aplomb than the more corpulent weight forward lines, but such picayunish delicacy is necessary on far fewer occasions than is the need for range, a more constant demand. Of course, with sinking lines the prettiness of presentation is a negligible factor.

Defenders of the double tapered lines point out that a double tapered line can be used for a considerable time, then turned the other way and used for an equal time. The suggestion is that one end wears down while the other end remains intact. I have not found this claim to be true. Fly lines do not so much wear out as they simply atrophy or meet with mishap. The back section, which spends most of its existence coiled around the reel spool, seems to spoil at about the same rate as the active portion of the line. Exposure to a variety of temperatures, bacteria, and eroding chemicals eventually leads to decomposition of the entire line. In other words, the effective life of weight forward lines is virtually the same as for double tapered lines.

There are a variety of other lines available, including slow sinking lines and floating sink-tip lines. Although these lines are all useful on occasion, the lake fisherman does not really require that much baggage. The deep areas of a lake can be well penetrated with a high density, fast sinking line. The shallow areas can be comprehensively covered from top to bottom with a floating line and a long leader. For example, if it is necessary to work a nymph across the floor of a shallow flat, simply extend the leader to 10 or 12 feet and use a moderately weighted fly. The floating line will allow a leisurely paced retrieval, while the nymph is puppeteered by the coy fisherman. The length of the leader and the weight of the nymph will determine the depth of the retrieve.

The technology of line making is constantly being improved, while the costs remain amazingly stable. Virtually any line that costs at least $15 is assuredly an excellent line. Be certain that your line number corresponds with the weight intended for your rod.

Casting a particular weight or size of nymph has less to do with using the "appropriate" gear than knowing what to do with the gear you have. Leader length and weight is often the key to modifying the performance capabilities of rod and line. With a 9 foot rod that balances with a 5 or 6 weight line, it is possible to cast convincingly virtually any weight or size of trout fly made. For example, a small, light nymph can be presented delicately on a bulbous weight forward line by attaching a long, fine tippet to the existing leader. An extremely heavy and bulky nymph can be turned over cleanly on the same equipment simply by altering the leader to a grossly foreshortened, but fast tapering mini-leader of 4 to 5 feet.

One of the most aggressive and successful nymph fishermen I know uses 4 to 6 foot, 6 to 8 pound test, level leaders. Sometimes, if he is feeling particularly cultivated and genteel, a passing mood, he will attach a 1 foot tippet of 5 pound test. He catches fish, many unwholesomely large, by casting far and often, or short and often. Basically he casts often, not leaving one molecule of water untroubled. He is a maniac and a dynamo, and comprehensive coverage is his secret.

Reels

Do not entertain for an instant buying a reel which costs less than $25.

A reel provides a place to neatly store the line, plus at least 100 feet of backing. In the case of playing large fish the reel also provides a definite mechanical advantage in collaboration with the leverage of the rod. A cheap reel is a liability and a handicap.

The difference between a cheap reel and an expensive one is largely a matter of smooth action versus a slightly distinguishable rougher action, light and convenient versus heavier and more awkward, and extremely durable alloy versus flawed, less resistant alloys. All of the qualities are relative, but, of course, over the long run a more expensive reel will be dependable, responsive and esthetically pleasing. A good reel complements a good rod.

Buy a reel which balances with the rod; this is a subjective judgment you should make by actually trying it on the rod. Make sure the reel suits the line. With at least 100 feet of backing, the line should nearly fill the reel spool, but not overflow. Select a reel which will accommodate interchangeable spools so that you may switch from one line to another with the least amount of fumbling. Finally, choose a reel that has a pleasing design, one that looks good and feels natural with your fly rod.

Automatic fly reels should be avoided like unemployed in-laws with degenerative leprosy. All automatic fly reels are automatic trouble. They are heavy, cumbersome, perversely unpredictable, and notoriously unresponsive. (Never buy anything that mounts sideways and needs winding.)

The control that it takes to land heavy, spirited fish is sometimes a delicate matter. The fly fisherman should always be directly "wired" to his rod and line. Clunky, moody fly reels interrupt the ideal union with a system of springs, gears, and housings which promise a host of calamities.

Reels should be tight and minimal, but micro-technically exact. Ultimately, the less machinery between the fisherman and the fish, the better.

An accumulation of the finest equipment and the development of casting artistry are not in themselves guarantees for slaying the fish. Fine casting is at best a secondary consideration. The primary factor employed in the successful pursuit of trout is a knowledge of lake ecology. A sloppy caster, an absolutely hopeless klutz, can and will catch fish if he has a well grounded knowledge of trout, trout habitat, and the basic aquatic life forms on the trout's menu. Once trout are located, the principal ingredient to success is the proper selection of the artificial and knowing how to emulate it.

The catching of fish perpetuates the refinement of all other aspects of the sport.

Chapter IV

Trout: Depth Perception

O scaly, slippery, wet, swift, staring wights,
What is 't ye do? What life lead? Eh, dull goggles?
How do you vary your vile days and nights?
How pass your Sundays?

Leigh Hunt

They pass their Sundays eluding us...though on rare occasions their wiles are few. Either way our obsessions are fed, and our minds flex compulsively in the awe of pursuit. The Irony. Man, the most complex and abstract of all animals, is snared in the awful passions of deceiving a cashew-brained and hairless beast.

Sometimes just after subduing the "stipple and rose mole" quarry, with the bubbles dying at my feet and the worn critter still bending, wrenching, we stare at each other, trout and man, and I wonder—which one of us most vacantly?

Still, this world is fraught with over-analysis and the distrust of the senses. As Robert Travers has suggested, perhaps fishing is a small form of rebellion. Our chasing after the "swift trouts diversified with crimson stains" (Pope) is an act of anti-urbanity; the intellect is best employed in subjects which transcend the "sensible".

Maybe a more rational explanation is lodged somewhere in the black recesses of a natural code. In lakes the fish is at the top of the food chain; it is king. Therefore, we must catch it—dethrone it, assert a mammalian dominance—that is the game. If another type of beast was at the top of this system of interlocking dependency, say a common species of aqua-dragon, we would be going "dragoning" rather than fishing. We would arm ourselves with winches, pulleys, block and tackle, and we would learn to splice cable rather than tie nail knots and blood knots. We would learn to dress grappling hooks and to cast with steel cranes.

Fortunately, we are not forced to such indelicacies. Many lesser species than dragons tickle our minds.

Is the trout a noble beast? What do we actually know of him? Surely the scientific should be no more exhaustive than the poetic.

No man can truly judge the nobility of an animal until he has felt it in and out, experienced it dying in his hands. Fish are the tangible stuff of dreams. Wild trout flare like bullets in the minds of fishermen. The death of each wild trout is a ceremony, a ritual, and a lesson. A wild trout should never be killed without an afterthought. It need not be repeated often.

The Northwest Indians believed that each animal lived again in the man who consumed it. A small sense of shame surely enriches the flesh.

Reflect a moment after you have killed a trout at lakeside, after you have rammed your stiff, cold fingers into the sticky cavity, zipping it open like a long, wet shoe... unfolding the entrails which hang like a knotted rope, exposing the runnel of meat like a slice of pink grapefruit. Observe the plier head, the flat-iron body. There is something to be learned from every feature.

A trout in the water is almost weightless, the nearly perfect union of an animal to its medium, yet liquid space suppresses movement. The trout's shape has been literally determined by the incompressibility of water. To overcome the resistance of water the fish must displace it; force it aside. Just as quickly the water closes again behind the wedgelike animal. The trout is of necessity a streamlined creature. The pointed head, the bulk forward, the body tapering to the tail...the combined design which allows movement with a minimum of turbulence. Trout are nature's waterborne missiles.

Fish do not swim by means of tail and fins. These are merely the steering apparatus and stabilizers, the elastic blades which prevent pitch and roll. Without fins the fish could swim, but its movement would be an erratic, directionless, crazy flight. The fish's propulsion comes instead from alternating waves of muscular contractions, first down one side, then the other. The rhythmic bending of the fish creates pressure points which push against the water like the action of skates on ice. Trout literally slide through the water, seeming to accelerate effortlessly on the current of their bodies.

The gills dangling at the end of the guts are raw red, echoing the blood which fills them. They are aligned like serrated crepe, a fluttering grillwork of tissue-thin lungs. The trout's circulatory system is simple and efficient, running in a direct line from the gills to the heart. Oxygen is filtered from the water as it billows through the gills. The oxygen is then transported by arteries directly into a two-chambered heart (a contrast to the complex four- chambered heart of mammals). Since the trout practically wears its lungs on its sleeve, the circulatory system is quite vulnerable. A finger shoved imprudently into a trout's delicate gills is surely as fatal (though less merciful) as a lead pipe across the skull.

Trout are equipped with highly attuned nostrils which lie in an almost direct line with the brain. The nostrils are strung tight with filaments of tissue like a radiator core. The trout's sense of smell is so keen that it also operates as a navigational device, following the subtle variances of a genetically coded environment. Foreign odors are instantly detected and are repugnant to the animal.

Trout are alerted by any unnatural noise or commotion which is telegraphed through the water. Noises in the air seem to have little effect on fish, but noises transmitted through the water or ground invariably trigger a sudden alarm. A shotgun fired in the air over fish will not disturb a fin. But allow an awkward movement on the bank or in a boat, and the fish will de-materialize in the glare of chaotic flight.

The trout's metallic-curtained flesh burns with an incandescence, but dies as an ember smothered when out of water. Even the hard-hearted are momentarily stunned by the brilliance of a wild trout, twisting on the line, breaking off shards of sunlight. It seems somehow esthetically appropriate that the nerve organs should be scattered over the entire surface of the fish, alive in the jeweled elegance. Trout are extremely sensitive to touch, but usually cease to struggle when cradled in a gentle and knowing grip. Escape is reflexive, but submission prevents injury in the dull hands of meddlesome beasts.

What of the popping, pressured eyes? Non-retractable, accusing, unlidded and staring even when they are not.

Trout have monocular vision; each eye collects a separate, uncoordinated image. In its two separate hemispheres of sight a trout sees a wide area extending to the sides and up and down. Its peripheral vision, although vague, is extensive. Straight ahead trout have a narrow area of binocular vision. This small area of coordinated vision is the most commanding. For that reason fish whirl to directly face what especially attracts them; the object of intense interest is held in the common field of both eyes.

It is debatable whether trout clearly distinguish colors. Microscopic examination of the nerve cells in the eye reveals a modest supply of visual cones, the nerve cells which differentiate between colors. Researchers are uncertain whether trout are reading the actual colors or the variety of shades implicit in the hues. It is quite possible that trout perception is basically limited to light intensities rather than colors.

The presence of visual rods in the trout's eyes are direct evidence of their night vision. Even though trout display poor visual acuity, they can detect movement and shape in the brightest or darkest of water.

Besides two bulbous and inefficient eyes, trout possess a mysterious lateral line, which runs the length of each slabbed side. Although little is known of this almost imperceptible seam, researchers have determined that the lateral line is central to the trout's non-visual navigation. With the constant aid of the lateral line trout avoid obstacles, wrinkling away in their own slipstream like spilled quicksilver. Trout negotiate without mishap the narrow channels and the obscure mazes of their underwater world.

The fisherman gropes above, in the broadest extremes of daylight, enacting clumsy pursuit, most often failing a convincing semblance of order, while the trout below gracefully performs the innate aqua-batics of a very stupid, but startlingly beautiful and sublime animal.

Chapter V

Flyfishing: Nymph O'Mania

"The pleasant'st angling is to see the fish—
Cut with her golden oars the silver stream,
And greedily devour the treacherous bait."

Shakespeare

A surface frenzy is the most arousing sight an angler can experience. However, a surface feed is a relative rarity. If you miss the hatch (the transformation of an insect from the larval form into winged adult) by hours or even minutes, you have missed the opportunity to confidently conspire to fish dry flies exclusively.

According to dry fly purists, nymph fishing is all wet. The literal accuracy of this opinion is indisputable.

Despite the somewhat less visual aspects of nymph fishing, most nymph fishermen will risk this esthetic deprivation for the sake of embracing the odds. It is a simple fact that more and larger fish are caught on nymphs than on any other class of fly. The explanation is obvious. Fish feed primarily on subsurface life forms because less than 10% of the life cycle of most aquatic insects is spent in the mature, airborne stage. In the course of the adult phase of the insects an even smaller percentage of time is spent in accessible range of fish. Like any other consumer, trout are subject to the dictates of supply and demand.

In nymph fishing, indeed in any fly fishing, there are no absolutes. There is good reason for this. We know very little about fish, and, because insects are even farther removed from the sphere of human empathy, we know deplorably less about them. However, the converse would destroy the sport. Absolute knowledge is the mortal enemy of enticement. Intrigue is the dominant element of any endeavor. Discovery is often anti-climatic, even if rewarding.

Despite the protests of the purists, who compare nymphing to fishing in a closet, not all nymph angling is a tug of war in the dark. Much nymphing takes place just under the barely ruffled surface of the lake. Many times I have stumbled upon the scene of trout wallowing and squirming in the skin of the lake. For all appearances, the trout were taking dry flies, but closer inspection proved the absence of a hatch. The trout were actually plucking out the nymphs suspended in the surface film of the lake like raisins floating in chablis.

This is not an infrequent occurrence, especially upon the pristine waters of alpine lakes. Because of the relatively short warm period and the resulting volatile growth brusts of both plants and animals in the summer, one form or another of larva can be found struggling for maturity at nearly all times in the upper, freshly warmed layers of the Spartan mountain lakes.

During these moments, with rapacious trout stalking life in the shallows, nymph fishing is as visually intriguing and explosive as any dry fly fishing. It is at these moments that precocious attempts at fly presentation must be suppressed. The subsurface feeders are wary and discerning customers.

Study your quarry, memorize its feeding pattern and cast the nymph at the proper moment. As Shakespeare once said, "Here comes the trout that must be caught with tickling."

It is imperative that one must take measured chances while nymphing. Cast quickly and boldly when the trout has veered away. If you have studied the fish's pattern of movement you can anticipate when and where it will return on the same course. In the meantime all vibrations in the cast line will have dampened and the nymph will be descending smoothly.

Use a long, fine tippet. It is far better to hook a fish and, perhaps lose it, than not to invite the jeopardy of a take at all. When the trout has the artificial in its window, allow the slightest pulse of movement to be imparted by a hand-twist retrieve. Slight movement may spur the trout's impulse before it has had time to closely scrutinize the fraud. If you have selected the nymph well, you will witness the fly disappear magically into the trout's maw.

Such moments hang in the fisherman's mind like the slow vapor of dreams.

Most of the larva indulged by trout are consumed outside of man's range of vision. Deep nymphing, although a required method for reticent trout, is rejected by many fly fishermen. Dragging a fly through the opaque depths has little appeal to those sportsmen who must be visually wired at all times to their craft. Despite the sensual inhibitions, deep nymphing is the single most productive form of angling, if not the most frustrating.

George Herbert stated three centuries ago, "You must lose a fly to catch a trout." If he were around today, he would surely be the only living patron saint of nymph fishermen.

You cannot catch trout, especially large trout, deep nymphing until you begin decorating lake bottoms with your precious collection of fur and feather. It's a simple but cruel rule.

If you feel matronly toward your flies, do not take up nymph fishing. Your life will be ruined before one season is ended.

The success of nymph fishing is directly contingent upon the proper selection of the nymph to be used in any given water. Fortunately, nymphs are a universal life form. Not only are they ubiquitous, but they are more or less homogenous to zones of latitude the world over. There are a number of major nymph orders which one can depend on finding in any fertile lake. The difficulty arises when one is confronted with the enormous variety of species within each order.

Although it is not necessary for an angler with a basic knowledge of larval forms to do a detailed study before actually catching fish, a higher rate of success will follow the angler who carefully observes his environment and painstakingly emulates the peculiar characteristics of the nymphs in particular waters.

The shape and general structure of nymph families rarely varies from lake to lake or region to region, but the sizes and colors within the species are multivarious. For example, the predominant dragonfly in one lake may be one inch long and dark green, while the basic dragon in another lake only a few miles away may be one and a half inches long and tawny brown. Such an undetected variance can completely sour the naive angler's efforts.

It is less important that the fisherman can identify specific species and impress himself with a battery of scientific jargon, than it is that he can observe and record important details. Scientific identification and the dropping of Latin names is a curious amusement; tying a reasonable facsimile of "whatever-it-is" is the heart of the matter.

Collecting nymphs in lakes presents obvious problems. Sheer depth is a prohibitive vault not apt to be violated by the common man. Although it is possible to assume the guise of an aberrant amphibian, complete with diving gear and collecting vials, few fishermen go to such extremes. For the patient man there are means and methods.

Seining through weed beds and silt is one way to capture a sampling. A small nylon net, cheesecloth, or a fiber glass window screen stretched across a wire frame, which is easily shaped out of a clothes hanger, will serve as a suitable seine. Larvae specimens can be netted at least haphazardly in shallow water. In deeper water the net cannot be controlled and is basically ineffective.

The autopsy method is another direct and productive approach.. A careful analysis of the stomach contents of sacrificed fish offers compelling and sometimes startling evidence of the larva in residence.

Dave Tolman, a fly fisherman possessing considerable knowledge and experience, is loathe to kill fish, but he shrewdly performs autopsies without compromising his values. I have been with Dave on a number of occasions when he has cunningly approached fishermen on the bank, admired their fish, exchanged pleasantries, and finally, gallantly and boldly offered to clean their catch. Although Dave has received some strange and suspicious glances, I have never seen his offer rejected. In the process of gutting the fish, he clandestinely performs the swiftest and most accurate stomach analysis this side of a police forensics lab.

Deductive reasoning is another method for studying larval forms. Begin by reading all the primary reference material on aquatic entomology that you can get your hands on. Once you have acquired a basic background and familiarity with the lake environment, logic becomes a reliable device. By studying the water conditions, the bottom type, weed contents and the mature insects which are in evidence, one can deduce a great deal about the larvae inhabiting a given water. Observe what is visible and you can accurately determine what is not visible.

Some fishermen keep shelves and cupboards stacked with labeled vials of preserved insects. I find this both slightly mercenary and unnecessary. Keep a small sketchbook and some colored pencils accessible. It requires little skill or effort to do a quick and basically accurate schemata of each larval form encountered. The sketchbook also provides a convenient medium for recording the time, place, depth and assorted information regarding the physical characteristics of the nymph and its environment.

Too many details are ultimately intimidating rather than helpful. I have found general impressions to be as reliable and as productive as file cabinets filled with alphabetized minutae.

Schwiebert's *Nymphs* is the most informative and painstakingly concise nymph study in print. The color plates, which have been sensitively reproduced, present an awesome array of graphic information. It is without doubt an authoritative and descriptive guide, but it is still just a guide. Despite the instructive ingredients of any book, the only reliable guide is your own two eyes. Train yourself to look...and look again. Every fisherman must develop his own discerning eye and cultivate his own total and inventive approach to the art of deceiving fish.

Do not let opportunities to observe the water environment elude you. Next time you are entranced in the hypnotic flicker of the campfire and perhaps the equally glazed companionship of fellow sportsmen, consider a lonely visit to the neglected periphery of night. Outside of the good natured but all too human noise of camp there is another world.

The galumping, splashing, and belching—the slurping, zinging, stinging, and stabbing sounds of the lakeside in darkness will envelop you. You will find yourself immersed in audio-exotica. But there is another universe too often neglected, the silent spaces of the lake. Study the vegetated shallows in the beam of a flashlight, and you will experience the nocturnal reverberations of a densely populated environ.

It is at night that the normally shy and retiring nymph populous becomes gregarious. Within the radius of the light beam a hundred luminescent and transparent larvae can be seen undulating in the occupation of predation and escape. There is no real zone of deference, no base of safety, no DMZ, no time out, no peaceful co-existence. Each creature is either pursuer or pursuant. It is a fixed, emotionless drama, but no less awful and riveting in its power than scripted theater.

Don't let the night slip by while hung in the plastic webbing of a lawn chair. Slip down to the water's edge and attend an aqua-drama choreographed in miniature.

Speculations on Emulations

The *American Nymph Fly Tying Manual* by Randall Kaufmann is the most comprehensive catalog of nymph patterns and tying instructions on the market today. For the avid nymph fisherman, it is an indispensible handbook and reference. However, it cannot be stressed too often that the studious and practical fisherman will deviate from the standard patterns and seek courses of his own experimentation and invention.

Along the way of my nymph fishing odyssey, I have developed certain attitudes, opinions, and biases concerning general principles of nymph construction. None of my opinions or anyone else's should be accepted as dogma or doctrine. Mull over and exploit those concepts which will instill the most confidence in your own creations.

Artificials fall into three general categories: the imitative, the impressionistic, and the expressionistic. Imitative patterns are based upon simulation and scientific accuracy. The problem that often arises in tying strictly detailed flies is that in capturing the scientific formalities, the creation becomes stiff and unyielding. The action is sacrificed for rote detail.

I believe that trout are most liable to drop their natural wariness and to succumb to temptation when confronted with a "buggy," fuzzy or ambiguous image rather than to something very distinct. It is easy to detect the faults in a clear image. A bad copy is an apparent counterfeit, while a shadowy illusion challenges doubt.

Impressionistic flies are more representative than imitative. They are purposefully vague in design with the intention of "suggesting" a variety of aquatic life forms. In duplicating a particular nymph the impressionistic design relies upon shape, color, and general features. In its final form an impressionistic fly should present a convincing illusion as opposed to an exact duplication of a particular larval form.

Expressionistic flies subordinate detail for the features which affect action. Any time the elements of a fly are stylized or exaggerated, including size, the tier has chosen to be expressive rather than imitative. The emphasis of expressionistic flies is on realistic movement or flamboyant design. Of course, the basic features, color, size and shape must exist in part to lend credence to the artificial. In my opinion a nymph pattern which moves unnaturally in the water is more apt to alert the fish than a nymph which lacks anatomic detail.

Charles Brooks points out in his book, *Nymph Fishing For Larger Trout,* that a somewhat blurred impression of the natural, coupled with lifelike movement, is all that is necessary for emulating the larger nymphs. Added features such as wing cases and antennae often result in disbalancing the nymph. Even in lakes all but the most perfectly balanced flies turn and twist in the water. Flat-bodied flies are especially prone to unnatural movement, wavering and fluttering uncontrollably on the retrieve.

All larvae, even those in the most turbulent rivers, maintain perfect equilibrium in the water. Their built-in gyro systems ensure constant upright locomotion.

By tying expressionistic flies in the "round" the fisherman creates the illusion from every angle that the fly is right side up and that its movement is natural. Water disturbance and twisted line are effectively counteracted by the even, circular identity of the nymph.

The natural, expressive action of a nymph depends in large part on the proper weighting of the fly and the position of the legs, which are commonly represented by long, soft hackle. No nymph pattern should be weighted near the butt of the hook as this induces an ungainly backsliding during the pauses on a retrieve. When a lot of weight is required on the fly, the lead wire should be evenly distributed in the front two-thirds of the nymph. When less weight is desirable, the lead wire should be wrapped tightly onto the hook shank in the thorax area. The correct positioning of the weight will cause the nymph to drop in a convincing manner during a dead sink. It is surprising the number of trout that will take during those seemingly lifeless moments. The fisherman who is alert to the slightest aberration in his line will hook many trout during the lull phase of the presentation.

On many patterns the movement of the legs can be enhanced by tying a stiff, dry fly quality hackle under the longer, more flexible, soft hackle. The underhackle holds the legs at right angles to the body and prevents the legs from plastering along the body of the nymph as it is towed through the water.

Despite the fact that many nymphs are anatomically proportioned with the legs protruding at intervals along the thorax region, almost all nymph patterns are hackled at the very front of the head. Ironically this is a physical detail which is often ignored by the scientifically-oriented fly tiers. I have found that the accurate positioning of the legs is more important than the length, the number, or the shape of the legs. The large, segmented nymphs are most convincing when hackled between the body and the head, or along the thorax region.

It is always judicious to thoroughly test prototype nymphs in clear water so that you can plainly see the effects and the defects of the design. (Warning: Do not test your creations while your wife is still in the bath.) Try every kind of retrieve from slow and smooth to rapid and erratic. The pedestrian activity of the nymph should approximate and conform to the style of movement of the order of larva you are representing.

Some Additional Considerations

Size:

For the most part the size of your artificial should nearly equal the actual size of the larva represented. Since aquatic insects often grow with the zest of adolescent children throughout the fishing season, the conscientious tier will concoct at least three consecutive sizes of each basic pattern.

Big, obscene, nasty-looking nymphs are sometimes startlingly effective, especially on the fat aristocrats which ignore every other conceivable pattern. At times it is advantageous to ignore scientific verity, to disregard the true size, the actual color, and the elements of definite shape. It often pays to exaggerate the size, to tamper with

26

attracting colors, and to simplify the design. For example, the most effective mosquito nymph that I have used is approximately three times as large as the brawniest mosquito larva that I have ever seen. I also find that consistently exaggerating the size of damselfly nymphs is a productive procedure. As a general rule (one that defies explanation) the larger the lake and the deeper the nymph is fished, the larger the nymph you can successfully employ. Upon an unpredictable number of occasions the proportions of the nymph used directly correlate with its productive properties.

Materials:

Whenever possible I prefer to use all natural materials, a romantic attitude fostered by an aversion to synthetics of all sorts. I am loathe to drag along too many of the discoveries of commercial enterprise into the heart of a naturalistic endeavor. By improvising it is possible to construct the bodies, over-cases, shellbacks and whatever without depending upon poly yarns, rubber foam, latex, plastic sheeting or any other of the plethora of laboratory "grown" petroleum derivatives. No doubt all of these materials are convenient, suitable and effective, but they personally do not appeal to me.

I find wire of various colors and weights to be a superior material for providing the flash and decorative embellishments on the body. Wire is not only cheaper but stronger than tinsel. Tinsel has the infuriating habit of breaking at crucial moments in the tying process. Wire has the same reflective properties as tinsel and can be wrapped tightly over the body of the nymph to create convincing segmentation. It also has the added advantage of providing weight to the nymph, sometimes eliminating the need to wrap strips of lead on the shank prior to dressing the fly.

Texture:

I tie virtually all of my nymphs, large and small, with dubbed bodies. I do this for the express purpose of creating slightly fuzzy, soft, pliable bodies. No nymph, despite the armored appearance of many, is brittle or crusty (with the exception of the cased caddis). Even the most fearsome of plated nymphs is flaccid and pulpy to the touch.

Trout have extremely sensitive mouths. I have found that a malleable, spongy body allows the fisherman a split second of grace to set the hook, while the taking trout is still sensing his error.

Generally, I use the twist and trim method of dubbing, especially on larger nymphs. It is a simple method involving a long loop of nymo tied in at the bend of the hook. The materials for dubbing, which may include feather fibers, fur, marabou, hair, or a combination thereof, are trapped between the parallel strands of the loop. Then the entire loop is pulled tight with hackle pliers clamped at the end. The hackle pliers are turned like a wind-up key, which twists the strands of the loop until the materials appear to have been braided together, but not so tight that the dubbing becomes knotted. The dubbing is then wrapped onto the hook shank in generous proportions. After it is tied off and secured, it has all the appearance of a motley nest for minute rodents. The body is then shaped and trimmed, the sophistication of design and coiffure being limited only by the artistic skills of the tier.

As mentioned earlier, I trim the fly so that it is rounded, a tapering cylinder from the tail to the thorax. Incidentally, the tail on most nymphs should be sparse and supple. In fact, it is a misnomer to refer to the organs at the rear of most larvae as tails at all. The soft protrusions at the rear are actually feather-like gills, the external lungs of the larvae.

For nearly all of the nymph bodies that I tie I choose materials which will produce a sheen at the edges. Loosely raveled materials are often superior because the frizzy fibers extending out from the body appear partially transparent, which produces the effect of an aura. It is this aura which suggests the transluscent qualities of most flies in their stages from larva to adult.

Each fly tier builds into his creations personal features which accommodate developed biases. Some of these features are based on observed details, experimentation and intuition; others are purely a form of artistic independence and identity...a signature.

The man hooked on nymphs is a lost soul.

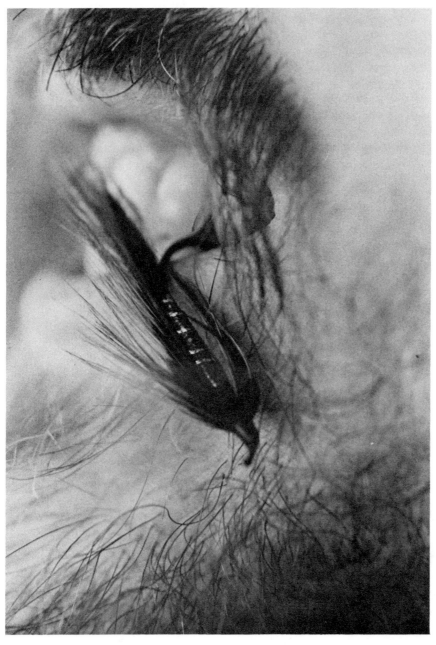

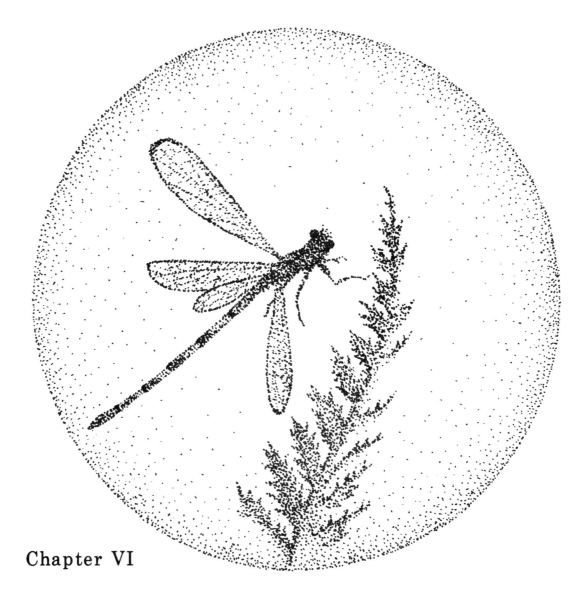

Chapter VI

Nymphs: Adolescents of the Deep

*"A snowy mountain
    Echoes in the
Jeweled eyes
    Of a dragonfly."*

> ...anonymous Japanese poet,
> 14th Century

Despite the lyrical, provocative beauty of the gossamer and velvet-winged adults, nymph fishermen literally owe their sport to the aquatic independence of a bunch of repulsive juveniles.

Hundreds of millions of years ago the remote ancestors of insects emerged from the sea and became air-breathers. They evolved in unending variety and spread to every distant corner of the earth, no matter how barren or how hostile. The land surfaces became crowded with the various life forms fighting to grab exclusive occupancy. Eventually, the lakes and streams offered the only refuge from the acute competition. As a result of the congestion,

29

many insects returned, step by step, to the rarified subterranean realms of a fluid real estate. Evolution had changed its mind.

Freshwater animal life, the insects and the fish, has resulted as a caprice of nature.

No known insect life is completely aquatic. Of the one million known insect species on earth only a few thousand are ever water dwellers. In their submerged environs insects live on borrowed time, until maturity liberates them to the air to mate, lay eggs, and die.

In the meantime the lakes offer an insulated environment. The balance of water temperature, oxygen in solution, food, and living space is particularly favorable in lakes. The relatively few insects that have adapted to subaquatic living thrive in great numbers. It is during their immature stages that they are completely adapted to life without air. Many freely forage the oxygen dissolved in water; others must rise to the surface to capture the air in their feathery fronds, or to trap oxygen bubbles in the hairy mesh on their bodies for later absorption, or to siphon the oxygen through beaks extended from the water into the air like converse straws.

Undoubtedly the best adapted to an aquatic existence are those insects which are equipped with gills. The dragonflies, damselflies, mayflies and caddisflies all possess closed tracheal systems, external gills which screen out the oxygen and diffuse the carbon dioxide. Because of their capacity to live and breathe in an entirely enclosed water environment these insects are a major available food source for fish and, consequently, the stuff of compelling mystery for fishermen.

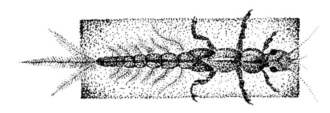

Mayflies: *Ephemeroptera*

Mayflies, bounding in clouds on their gossamer wings or sailing across the water like competitors in the Victoria Regatta, are the fairy creatures of the wetlands. The adults are delicate beyond belief. Their wings are micro-thin and flimsy and their legs spindly, too weak for walking. The adult mayfly's disused digestive system is pumped up with air for added flight-worthiness. Life is transitory for adult mayflies, lasting from a few hours to, at most, a few days. The mayfly is a fragile insect incapable of defense, yet it has endured for 250 million years and has obsessed fishermen for the last 500 years.

Although the several hundred species of mayflies are of minor importance in the overall insect world, their importance is major in the water world. They are prolific and are subject to wide predation, overabundance acting as a hedge against constant rout. The nymphs which survive savaging may spend up to two years on a lake bottom, molting possibly 30 times. Their size and coloration is endless, although the most common sizes range from 8-22 (hook sizes for reference) and they are usually colored predominantly subdued blue-grays, earth greens, or light browns.

The mayfly is literally a nymph for all seasons. There is a mayfly nymph for every kind of water and every condition.

Most mayflies are distinguished by seven pairs of oval-shaped gills distributed along the body. Many also have gills composed of three fern-like fibers at the tip of the abdomen. The thorax is usually approximately one-third of the overall length of the nymph. The three pairs of limbs common to all insects are distributed along the thorax, ending just behind the eyes on most species.

Mayfly nymphs are either crawlers, burrowers, free swimmers, or clingers. In their varied activities these nymphs forage bits of organic matter too small to interest other water dwellers, but in their abundance are themselves star attractions for other foragers. Owing to their variegated characteristics, including locomotion, there is no single recommended method for fishing the nymph. I have surmised, however, that a dead drift, followed by a hand-twist retrieve is the single most productive technique.

Experimentation is always the best policy.

Timberline (represents a wide variety of brownish gray mayfly nymphs, impressionistic). Pattern by Randall Kaufmann. Sizes 12-16, weighted slightly. This is a mayfly nymph of universal appeal. It is usually fished along the bottom with enticing twitches, or dead drift in the top layer of the lake.

Thread:	Brown.
Tail:	Three moose body hairs, tied short.
Rib:	Copper wire.
Body:	Hare's ear fur, clipped directly from the ear, guard hairs left in, dubbed.
Wingcase:	Dark side of ringneck pheasant tail.
Thorax:	Same as body, generously proportioned.
Legs:	Sparsely tied ringneck pheasant tail fibers.

Timberline Emerger (mayflies of the alpine lakes, impressionistic). Pattern by Randall Kaufmann. Sizes 10-14. An all-purpose mayfly emerger intended for use in the mountain lakes of the West.

Thread:	Gray (black, brown and yellow are also suitable).
Tail:	Three black moose body hairs.
Body:	Mixture of 30% muskrat and 70% gray seal (light brown and dark green fur mixtures are also acceptable), dubbed.
Wing:	Grizzly hackle tip, tied short.
Hackle:	Two turns of brown tied back.

Greenhead (a nondescript mayfly, expressionistic). Pattern by Donald Roberts; a variation on Kaufmann's Timberline and Trueblood's Shrimp. Sizes 8-16, from light to heavily weighted. Because of its breathing, pulsating action and ambiguous appearance, this is the most broadly suggestive mayfly pattern available.

Thread:	Green.
Tail:	Fibers from a grouse flank feather.
Body:	Light or medium gray muskrat fur, dubbed generously and trimmed.
Thorax:	Same as body, but larger.
Hackle:	Grouse flank feather, teased back, tied sparsely.

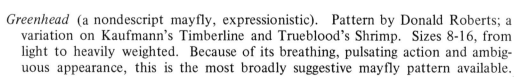

Black and White (very dark mayflies, expressionistic). Pattern by Donald Roberts. Sizes 8-22, from light to heavily weighted. This pattern does not closely represent any known mayfly nymph, yet its expressive qualities are especially enticing near nightfall and on dark, rainy days in lowland lakes. I like to drift this nymph slowly along rock ledges and basalt cliffs near the surface in the evening. It is almost always taken with considerable force.

Thread: Black.

Tail: Fibers from guinea fowl feather.

Body: Black seal fur, dubbed loosely.

Thorax: Continuation of body.

Hackle: A soft, guinea fowl saddle or neck feather.

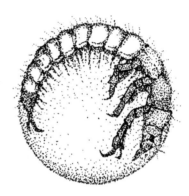

Caddisflies: *Trichoptera*

Trichoptera is an apt and descriptive Greek word meaning "hairy wings". Caddis, the common name, is a Celtic term meaning "heavy cotton twill". In its sand and gravel case the caddis larva does indeed look like a gentleman insect well fitted in corduroy. At least 750 kinds of the clandestine caddis have been identified, and there are surely more which have eluded the files and vials of entomologists.

Every fisherman can be assured that a member or two of the caddis clan, the largest group of aquatic insects, inhabits each and every body of water that is fishable. They are found to occupy every bottom type, and where conditions are particularly favorable, they populate in dense ghetto communities. To offset a high mortality rate each adult female lays from 300-1,000 eggs, which are enclosed in a gelatinous matrix. The larvae are almost without exception bottom dwellers, and most construct their own portable hovels from a variety of available debris. These shy insect craftsmen are spinners and masons; beginning with the manufacture of a weblike silk tube, they complete their cases with a mortared layer of pebbles, sand, twigs, gravel or vegetation. Different species of caddis fortify with different materials. Several caddis cases have been found to contain gold dust, nuggets, and other semi-precious gems.

For the nymph fisherman the real gold is found in the several species of caddises which are multibrooded, hatching sporadically throughout the season. The caddis pupa, the freshly hatched adult which has shucked its pupal case, rises quickly to the surface and with barely a pause begins its airborne career.

32

The caddis pupa is like a wet cat; not a pretty creature, but rather hairy and motley. The pupa is usually dull in coloring, although there are some species which are bright orange and another which is striking green. Dusky browns, grays and tans are the most common and therefore the most practical to emulate. The floozy, unfortunate appearance of the pupa can be attributed to the long, gangly legs, folded under wings, and hundreds of gill filaments which cover the body surface like rough, dusty lacework. Caddis larvae also have rectal gills, but these are barely visible and are, therefore, negligible to the fly tier.

Since the rising pupal form inspires the most enthusiastic of trout seiges, it makes good sense to copy the gesture, to sink the nymph to the bottom before beginning the retrieve. Then strip in line fairly quickly and smoothly until within two or three feet of the surface. Pause dramatically and finish with a classic Leisenring Lift.

Moose Mane (cased caddisflies, imitative). Pattern by Donald Roberts. Sizes 8-16, long shank, heavily weighted. This fly can be lethal in the early season, fished dead drift where streams flow into lakes and reservoirs. If the nymph does not remain on the bottom, it will not receive even passing interest.

Thread:	Black.
Tail:	Optional; red feather fibers, very short and sparse.
Body:	Moose mane, spun on in the manner of deer hair and clipped to a tubular shape.
Thorax:	Continuation of body.
Hackle:	Short but supple furnace hackle.

Unkempt (an emerging caddis, expressionistic). Pattern by David Tolman. Sizes 8-22, from no weight to heavily weighted. This nymph is tied as a fuzzy ball, totally devoid of specific details. It is probably suggestive of a variety of larvae. Different tones of brown and gray can be achieved by clipping the fur from different areas of the hare's mask. Both the dead drift and Leisenring Lift are productive methods.

Thread:	Black or brown.
Tail:	None.
Body:	Hare's mask, dubbed heavily, guard hair left intact.
Thorax:	Continuation of body.
Hackle:	None.

Little Green Caddis (a pupal stage of caddis, imitative). Pattern by Charles Brooks. Sizes 12-16, 1X long. This fly can also be tied with a dark gray body. Both the gray and green caddis are found in silt and gravel areas. It is a crawler and should be fished very slowly across the bottom, except when emerging, then use the Leisenring Lift.

Thread:	Olive or black.
Tail:	None.
Egg Sac:	Tuft of fluorescent green yarn.
Rib:	Gold wire.
Body:	Hunter's green yarn.
Thorax:	Tan or gray ostrich herl.
Wings:	Ostrich herl tied back.
Hackle:	Grouse body feather.

Cream Caddis (an uncased caddis larva, imitative). Pattern by Charles Brooks. Sizes 8-14, unweighted. This caddis nymph should be fished to simulate as closely as possible the behavior of emergent nymphs. It is also an excellent feeler fly for shallow bays and inlets.

Thread:	Tan or brown.
Tail:	None.
Rib:	Fine copper wire or brown or olive thread.
Body:	Creamy tan fur or yarn.
Thorax:	Gray or black ostrich herl.
Hackle:	Dyed black hen, soft fibers, tied short and sparse.

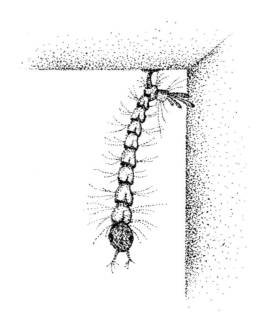

Mosquitoes: *Diptera*

During the early season it is not only hardheaded but foolhardy to bear a grudge against Mr. Mosquito; after all, only the female of the species bites. In many lakes and reservoirs, especially the alpine variety, mosquitoes begin emerging even before the ice has cleared. At these times the mosquito assumes the role of special entree on the menu. In some mountain lakes the mosquito remains a constantly patronized food source throughout the season.

Although mosquito hatches rarely trigger trout feeding festivities, there are occasions when emergent mosquitoes command exclusive interest. During these moments, a dry imitation, regardless of how attractive to the fisherman, is a futile fraud, at least until it becomes soggy enough to sink. The trout, occupied with engorging on the larvae in the surface film, rarely look higher.

Most mosquito pupae move freely in their underwater environment. Some are capable of siphoning oxygen from aquatic plants. Others, equipped with the capacity to expand their bodies into buoyant balloons, rise to the surface to breathe. They are endowed with a snorkel arrangement for breathing, a tube that penetrates through the surface film into the air. A collar of greasy hair on the snorkel expands to lock the insect in place. Even during the most windswept and rough water days trout can often be seen hooking down mosquito larvae from the liquid rafters.

Even though mosquito larvae are characteristically rather small, trout on the whole do not seem dubious of exaggerated imitations. The various mosquito species are also fairly uniform in color. The attractive gray and white striped thorax is the dominant feature of all mosquito imitations.

Upon many an occasion mosquitoes have fulfilled the paradoxical role of both curse and cure of an otherwise fishless outing.

Emergent Mosquito (mosquito pupa, imitative). Pattern by Randall Kaufmann. Sizes 12-18. This nymph is usually fished dead drift in the surface film.

Thread:	Black.
Tail:	Three short fibers of black moose body hair.
Body:	Stripped peacock herl over slight taper of dark fur.
Wings:	Two grizzly hackle tips tied short over the thorax.
Thorax:	Peacock herl.
Hackle:	None.

Public Enemy No. 1 (mosquito larvae, expressionistic). Pattern by Donald Roberts. Sizes 8-16, long shank, weighted. This is a utilitarian feeler pattern for working in, around, over and under the snags and debris along the edges of alpine lakes. Allow the fly to sink, then retrieve it with staccato twitches, followed by considerable lulls. The least disturbance in the line is indication of a take. The angler must be acutely aware of the posture of his line at all times.

Thread:	Black.
Tail:	Grizzly hackle fibers tied short and sparse.
Body:	Stripped grizzly hackle, tied in fine end first.
Wings:	Two grizzly hackle tips tied extremely short.
Thorax:	Black ostrich herl or green peacock herl.
Beard:	Soft gray deer hair or squirrel tail, extending to the hook point, sparse.

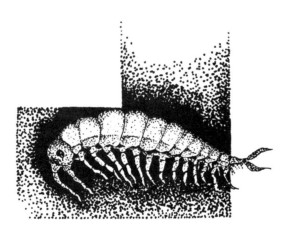

Shrimps and Scuds *(Crustaceans),* **Sowbugs** *(Asellus),* **and Crawfish** *(Astacidac)*
I have lumped all of the above creatures together because they are not insects, yet they are invaluable to the nymph fisherman. Each of these animals belongs to a class of invertebrates in the *phylum Arthropoda.* Although each of these animals

vary in color and size, and somewhat in shape, all share similar environments, and all have similar habits. Within each order there is little necessity to make painstaking identification of the species. Generalities often provide the most serviceable information to the fly tier.

Where these creatures are abundant, they are a high protein food source which is often reflected in the size and condition of the fish. All but the crawfish are found almost exclusively in weedy areas with a fine silt bottom. The true freshwater shrimp is a relative rarity which can be, for all practical purposes, completely ignored.

Among scuds, often erroneously referred to as shrimp, the *Hyalella* is the most common and is found in nearly all shallow, weedy lakes. *Gammarus,* the larger specie of scud, is not so well distributed, but in those waters where it is found it is the virtual mainstay of the trout's diet. In many alkaline lakes found in the western states, scuds are so abundant that I have seen large trout display total disdain and disinterest during mayfly and caddisfly hatches.

Usually where scuds are found, so are the dull and lowly sowbugs. Like their counterparts on land, they are dark, squat and communal. It is hard to imagine a creature more featureless and drab, yet the sowbug redeems itself by sheer availability which knows no season. The sowbug is as good a pattern in winter as it is in summer.

The advantage of all of these primitive animals is that they are similar in appearance and are easily expressed in design. Small, fuzzy, nondescript flies tied in a variety of greens, yellows and browns usually prove sufficient. All are active foragers and move about with erratic abandon, scuttling to and fro in the subaquatic jungles. And there lies the crux of the problem in fishing the crustaceans.

How does one adequately probe weed beds? There is no single solution which can translate into simple directions. Suffice it to say that the experienced and resourceful angler will find the channels and the pockets where different methods and approaches can be tested.

Crawfish are esteemed for their delicate flavor as much by fishermen as by fish. They are found scurrying along lake bottoms in depths of 10 to 30 feet and are always a highly regarded windfall by large trout on the stalk. They move backwards in swift, erratic spurts, a motion which is most effectively simulated by long, rapid strips of line.

Crawfish, like many other creatures of the deep, assume colors which are reflective of their environment. Subdued greens, browns and grays are the most commonly occuring colors which tint their sheet-metal hides. Crawfish are dedicated scavengers and are therefore found scouting up and down the food shelves in lakes.

Come to think of it, the dedicated angler is not dissimilar in habit.

Trueblood Shrimp (general scud pattern, expressionistic). Pattern by Ted Trueblood. Sizes 8-16, weighted. A fly for any depth and any occasion; it is just plain "buggy".

Thread:	Brown.
Tail:	Brown partridge feather fibers.
Body:	A mixture of otter and cream seal, dubbed loosely.
Thorax:	Continuation of body, fibers teased out.
Beard:	Brown partridge fibers, three-fourths the length of the hook.

Ghost Bug (light colored or clear-bodied scuds, expressionistic). Pattern by Dave Tolman. Sizes 8-22. This pattern is most worthwhile fished in the weedy shallows, especially in the very early morning. It should be crept through cover and vegetation, or along basalt rubble. It probably imitates a number of other larvae besides scuds.

Thread:	Black.
Tail:	Grizzly hackle fibers.
Body:	White rabbit fur dubbed and trimmed.
Rib:	Silver wire, or tinsel.
Thorax:	Continuation of body.
Wing:	Grizzly hackle fibers tied very short and sparse.
Hackle:	White hen, supple and sparse.

Chrome Bug (general scud and sowbug pattern, expressionistic). Pattern by Donald Roberts. Sizes 8-22, weighted. I have found that the almost metallic sheen of seal fur creates a transluscence especially suited to the subaquatic species. The two colors noted below are favored, but any number of others are also useful.

Thread:	Green or red.
Tail:	None.
Body:	Dubbed seal fur, dyed insect green or maroon, back trimmed, belly fibers teased out to represent appendages.
Thorax:	Continuation of body.
Hackle:	None.

Giant Crawfish (crawfish, expressionistic). Pattern by Donald Roberts. Sizes 2-10, weighted. This fly is intended for the larger, carnivorous trout and should be maneuvered right along the bottom in rock rubble, snags, debris and all the most exasperating locations. This fly is never a red-hot item, but, when it is taken, the fish is invariably large, and the action is awesome.

Thread:	Black or brown.
Tail:	None.
Body:	Reddish brown chenille, tapered toward the eye of the hook, overlaid with coyote tail hair or long, soft deer hair.
Thorax:	Continuation of body, larger near the bend of the hook.
Hackle:	Several turns of long, supple badger over the entire body.
Pincers:	Coyote tail hair or deer hair, tied in a "V" equal to body length.

Seaweed's Crawdad (crawfish, impressionistic).   Pattern by Seaweed (Marshal) Escola. Sizes 8-16, weight optional. This pattern is regarded favorably without bias by spiny ray as well as trout. Despite the fact that crawfish are bottom dwellers, this pattern can be lethal fished just under the surface.

Thread:	Black.
Tail:	Pheasant tail fibers, trimmed short and square over the eye of the hook.
Body:	Dark green chenille, tapered toward the tail, overlaid with pheasant fibers.
Thorax:	Continuation of body, larger than tail area, situated near the bend of the hook.
Hackle:	Furnace hackle, several turns over the thorax area.
Pincers:	Pheasant tail fibers, tied in a "V" at the bend of the hook.

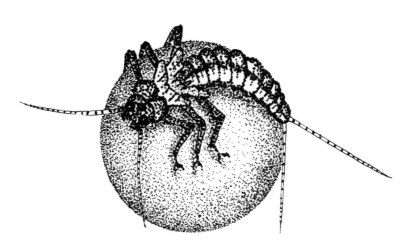

Stoneflies: *Plecoptera*

It is the rare breed of stonefly that can survive in still water. All but the most obscure of species demand the constant turmoil and vital aeration of swift waters for their propagation and proliferation. Yet the stonefly is not to be discounted as a lake nymph.

My adherence to this attitude is not a product of sheer perversity, nor is it borne out of entomological ignorance. I initially discovered the value of the stonefly nymph as a searcher pattern for lake fishing in a rather oblique manner. I had been working the Burnt River in Eastern Oregon. It was early June, and the California species of stonefly was rather evident, yet inactive. My studied and regionally accurate imitation was not turning a head. I reasoned that the trout were awaiting the mass creeping migration characteristic of the species. Less than two miles upriver Unity Reservoir, an irrigation scheme which interrupts the pastoral meandering of the Burnt River, awaited my attention.

I broke down my rod, with the big nymph still attached, and drove up to the reservoir. I never did get back to the river that day, as the stonefly nymph, which I had been too lazy to replace, dredged up one hefty rainbow after another.

This tangential discovery led me to experiment in numerous other lakes at odd times of the year. The results have been too consistent, if not bizarre, to ignore.

The cryptic, loathsome appearance of the stonefly nymph is deceiving. It is the gentle giant of the water world; it is a vegetarian and a pacifist. None of the nearly 500 species identified in North America can swim, but are confined to crawl about on rock and boulder-strewn stream bottoms, passively grazing on aquatic flora.

There is no mistaking this hideous river denizen; its features are all too obvious, consistent, and distinctive, despite a variety of coloration which spans the spectrum of nature's palette. In a general sense, grays, yellows, browns and greens dominate the stonefly's apparel. The single most identifying feature of the stonefly is the three, overlapping, plated sections over the thorax. The stonefly's ample body is constructed of ten segments as clearly ribbed as flexible conduit. All stoneflies, regardless of model, come equipped with a slightly demonic forked tail. The stonefly's fuzzy gills are located on the undercarriage of the thorax. Since the nymph inhabits waters with a current, its legs are relatively long and stout. At the end of their usual one-year life cycle, the nymphs emerge by hoisting themselves out of the water onto rocks, vegetation or any available object. I have seen great numbers of split nymphal shucks clinging with skeletal persistence to the bleak, rusted shells of dead automobiles, the half-submerged monoliths of industry nose down in a river grave.

The stonefly nymph's effectiveness in lakes is not really an enigma. A part of its success can be attributed to the highly expressive qualities of the imitation. While these patterns do not closely resemble any of the larval forms normally found in lakes, they are so ambiguous and so ostentatious as to actually fit the category of nymph-lure. The theatrical aspects of these bright nymphs should establish their reputation more as attractors than as simulators of actual nymphs.

Regardless of the philosophical basis for the nymph patterns used, the angling method should conform to the actual habits and movements of the species. The single most productive approach is to fish the stonefly along the bottom and to retrieve it by a painfully slow inching process.

If you have the faith and the inclination to experiment with the stonefly nymph in complacent waters, do not pessimistically dwell on the nature of reality. After all, illusion is the substance and the currency of any art.

Lakestone (stonefly nymph, highly expressionistic). Pattern by Donald Roberts. Sizes 8-12, long shank, weighted. I tie this pattern in several different colors, but adhere to the same basic principles for each. I suggest the two color schemes below because of their iridescence.

Thread:	Black or green.
Tail:	Pheasant tail fibers tied in a "V".
Body:	Pink marabou, dubbed and trimmed in the round—or light gray muskrat.
Rib:	Single strand of brown wool and copper wire—or single strand of green wool and silver wire.
Thorax:	Black ostrich herl or green peacock herl.
Hackle:	One long grizzly and one long badger, several turns over herl—or long, red dyed hen hackles.

Golden Girl (stonefly nymph, expressionistic). Pattern by Donald Roberts. Sizes 6-12, weighted, up-eye hook. This fly should be fished deeply for trout, but shallowly for spiny ray, which often take it with homicidal force.

Thread:	Yellow or brown.
Tail:	Pheasant tail fibers tied in a "V".
Body:	Brown rabbit fur, dubbed and trimmed in the round.
Rib:	A single strand of brown wool alternated with green thread and gold wire.
Thorax:	Black ostrich herl or green peacock herl.
Hackle:	One long grizzly and one long badger, several turns over herl.

Water Bugs and Beetles: *Hemiptera*

Fewer than 200 subspecies of this ancient aqua-family exist today, although they are abundant in every type of water from turbulent to dead still, from nearly opaque to transparent, from tepid to frigid. These creatures rarely attract trout into foolish spectacles of consumption, but are a constant and mundane staple of the trouts' diet. It is the exception when a fish's stomach does not reveal one variety or another of water bug mixed into the remaining digestive pulp, like the seeds in strawberry jam.

All of the waterbugs, regardless of size, are voracious predators. They are also quite gregarious, writhing in intimate communities, sharing in the social confusion. Most of the beetles must remain in constant, erratic motion when submerged. If they pause for even a moment, they will bob back to the surface, buoyed by the oxygen trapped in their hairs and beneath their wingcases, which function as refillable oxygen tanks.

The water strider, water boatman, back swimmer and assorted nondescript beetles are not deep divers. They spend their lives thrashing about in the near surface environ. *Belostomatidae*, the giant water bug, is an exception. The giant water bug, which may grow to over four inches long, is the most powerful of all insect hunters. Its venom allows it to subdue and devour other insects, snails, worms, leeches, tadpoles, small fish and frogs. Because of its treacherous abilities, the giant water bug is sometimes a dreaded pest in fish hatcheries.

The ability of many kinds of water bugs to fly may be a mechanism to escape drought; otherwise there appears to be little reason for their airborne faculties. Giant water bugs sometimes leave the water and fly about on impulse, an action with no known intent.

Water striders rarely use their wings, preferring instead to take part in spirited, ivy league style races. Sculling away in a blur of motion, they row with nervous quickness but never actually break the skin of the water.

Another relative, the water boatman, also has wings but prefers to spend its time beneath the surface of the water, darting about intimidating everything from small larvae to fish ten times its size.

It seems predictable that nature in her own time will surely trim the disused wings from many species of the water bug.

In general, water bugs and beetles are dark colored creatures. They are basically uniform in shape, tapering down from the head, and fairly scruffy in appearance, especially underwater, where air bubbles coat them like a milky froth. Almost without exception, the various species of water bugs are equipped with long, powerful, oarlike legs for pumping through the fabric of their underwater world.

When tying water bug and beetle patterns there is little need to study and emulate fine detail. Basic green, brown, or black provide the full range of necessary color. The beetles need little or no hackle. The predacious and highly mobile water bugs, on the other hand, should be tied with long, soft hackle to denote the legs. In any case, simplicity is the essence of design.

The value of these amorphous creatures should not be discounted. Many large trout have been "bugged" to death.

Zug Bug (water bugs and beetles, probably a myriad of larvae, impressionistic). Sizes 10-32. This is an all purpose searcher pattern. When all else fails the Zug Bug may offer salvation. The Zug Bug is usually tied with a wing, but I prefer to use a soft hackle instead.

Thread:	Black.
Tail:	Peacock sword fibers.
Body:	Peacock herl.
Rib:	Silver wire.
Thorax:	Continuation of body.
Hackle:	Grouse flank feather, tied short and sparse.

Aqua-Bug (water beetle, impressionistic). Pattern by Donald Roberts. Sizes 10-22. Retrieve this nymph slowly, but keep it nervous. Interrupt with a dead pause every few feet. Be alert to the slightest movement in the line, indicating a "sipping" take.

Thread:	Black.
Tail:	None.
Body:	Black seal fur, brown hackle trimmed close.
Shellback:	Optional; brown partridge fibers or pheasant tail fibers pulled tightly over the back.

Giant Water Bug (giant water bug, expressionistic). Pattern by Donald Roberts. Sizes 2-10, weighted. This fly should be fished with a high density line and a short leader. Keep your cast high to avoid, if not crude acupuncture, a glancing concussion. Black bass, brown trout and, presumably, alligators are susceptible to this gross creation, especially at nightfall. This fly is never just taken; it is "mugged".

Thread:	Brown.
Tail:	None.
Body:	Brown or black seal fur, a scraggly mass.
Thorax:	Continuation of body.
Hackle:	Pheasant rump feather, long and soft with a green or amber sheen.

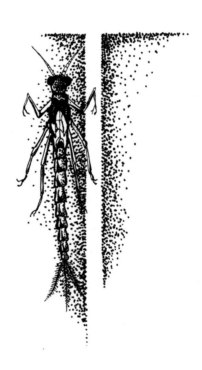

Damselflies: *Odonata*

Tennyson referred to the delicate damselfly's wings as "clear plates of sapphire mail." It is indeed the prettiest of all aquatic insects. It is also an important food source for trout.

To the uninformed, an adult damselfly looks like a small dragonfly. They are of the same order, and their habits are similar. But to the nymph fisherman they are a very different breed of cat, easily distinguished by their size, their wing positions, and their eyes. Damselflies are more petite than their more contentious brethren. The dragonfly nymph is a squat and stocky critter, while the damselfly is long and smoothly contoured. An adult dragonfly at rest holds its wings in a horizontal position. The damselfly rests with its wings folded in a vertical position. The dragonfly's eyes are larger and cover more of the head, while the damselfly's eyes are set apart, to the sides of the head.

All *Odonata* begin life as tiny eggs deposited in fresh water. The minute creature that emerges from the egg is called a *naiad* and bears very few features reminiscent in the adult. A damselfly *naiad*—or nymph—may spend from one to three years as an underwater resident. During this prolonged juvenile period, it molts from 10-15 times, growing larger with each successive shedding. While residing in its liquid atmosphere, the damselfly nymph breathes through gills and carries on a very active existence of predation.

This slim, brown or dark green creature is aided in its hunting endeavors by a very specialized labium which is common to dragonflies as well. The labium is elongated and hinged, with strong grasping jaws at the end. It is carried folded back with the scoop-shaped front held masklike over the face. When prey comes within range, the labium is shot forward to grasp the victim. Besides having a portable trap extending from the mouth, the *Odonata* also have excellent vision to aid in hunting, mating and escape. Each eye may contain as many as 30,000 facets, each facet equipped with its own retina and lens, enabling almost 360° of vision.

The damselfly nymph spends its days concealed in silt and weeds, the eyes barely protruding and the jaw poised, waiting to ambush an unsuspecting nymph, even its own kind. Sometimes it roams a territory hoping to flush out a startled mosquito, its main staple and favored course. When alarmed, for example when caught in the sights of a dragonfly nymph, the damselfly dives abruptly for the camouflage and cover of vegetation and muck.

Prodigious numbers of damselfly nymphs emerge sporadically on their final journey to adulthood. Hatches occur throughout the entire season. When they are especially available, trout seem hopelessly gullible and can hardly resist a well-presented imitation. I would count the attractive and graceful damselfly nymph as the most rewarding and provocative of all shallow water flies.

Damselfly Nymph (damselfly nymph, impressionistic). Pattern by Seaweed (Marshal) Escola. Sizes 10-16. This fly is most effective fished dead drift in the surface film, but I have used it with convincing results in every strata of the lake.

Thread:	Brown.
Tail:	Green-dyed grizzly hackle tip.
Body:	Variegated green yarn.
Thorax:	Green yarn tied in a small bunch on the top.
Hackle:	Green-dyed hen or grizzly hackle, sparse and supple.

Heather Nymph (damselfly nymph, impressionistic). Pattern by Fenton Roskelly. Sizes 10-16, long shank, slightly weighted. This and every other damselfly nymph should be weighted at the thorax; when the movement of the line is arrested, the nymph will dive as if startled, a natural response to a cruising fish. Use with a long, light tippet to encourage free, lifelike movement.

Thread:	Black.
Tail:	Red hackle fibers.
Body:	Insect green seal fur.
Rib:	Gold wire.
Thorax:	Peacock herl.
Hackle:	Grizzly, sparse and supple.

Black Collar (damselfly nymph, expressionistic). Pattern by Donald Roberts. Sizes 8-16, weighted in the thorax region. This fly is more ambiguous and a lot less scientific than most other damselfly patterns. Although it is less detailed, it imparts a breathing action which must either attract or infuriate passing trout. It is an indispensable pattern in the lowland lakes.

Thread: Black.
Tail: None.
Body: Brown seal fur, dubbed and trimmed.
Thorax: Black seal fur, a shaggy mane.
Hackle: Pheasant rump feather, copper or ginger sheen.

Dragonflies: *Odonata*

In the Oriental countries the dragonfly inspires artistic admiration and mystical reflection. It is regarded as a creature of both power and charm, an image which often contrasts sharply to the satanic folklore assigned this perplexing insect in the western world. Despite the nature of man's mythological assumptions, in its own realm it is an awesome and magical animal.

In its magificently attired adult stage, but more significantly, in its motley nymph form, the dragonfly is an integral cog in the ecological machine. It is a fierce beast, the conqueror of its own insect kingdom. After all, it is impossible to consider a creature that is magnificent but harmless, that is the mosquito's dreaded enemy, and that is of primary importance in the trout's diet, as anything but an incredible windfall.

As a youngster the dragonfly's aggressiveness is entirely food oriented. As a glorious adult, sex accounts for its bellicose behavior. On both counts the dragonfly is counterpart to man, and is regarded with respect and affection by artists, ascetics and nymph fishermen.

The dragonfly is a ubiquitous creature, existing in every region from tropical to sub-arctic. It is so well represented in the temperate zone that in early spring on western waters the dragonfly nymph is often the exclusive item in the aqua-larder.

Dragonfly nymphs vary from one inch to over three inches long. Every species is clearly segmented between the thorax and the body, a feature which is often ignored by amateur and professional tiers alike. The colors range from green to purple in the

44

bright hues and from dull yellow to mottled brown in the subdued spectrum. Relative to overall body size, dragonflies have very long legs. The general shape of the nymph is perhaps the single most important element in producing an effective pattern. In the early season the nymphs are squat and rotund. The head is always large, lion-like, and the body varies from a thick, thumb shape in the spring to a uniform, tubular shape as the nymph nears emergence.

The dragonfly nymph is both the slowest and the fastest moving nymph found in fresh water. Normally a very languid hunter, relying on stealth and camouflage for each ambush, it spurts forth with deceptive speed when quarry comes within range, capturing anything from larvae to small fish in its hinged, spring-loaded mandibles.

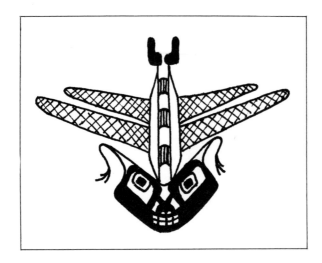

In fishing the dragonfly nymph a slow retrieve should be employed to suggest the usual sluggish movement, occasionally interspersed with a surge to imitate the sudden rapid propulsion of the nymph shooting forward by expelling a jet of water from its anal opening.

Although there are a number of painstakingly scientific patterns available, they are for the most part as rigid as plastic replicas. The dragonfly nymph must pulsate to be plausible. The answer is to rely on a highly expressive and pulpy design.

Rosenbaum's dragonfly nymph is a good example, which, according to Squeak Rosenbaum of Rosenbaum's Flies in Baker, Oregon, was first brought to him by a truck driver from Spokane. Polly Rosborough's nondescript, which Polly credits as original to Jim Chase, is similar to Rosenbaun's nymph in style and shape, but differs in color, tending to be of a lighter hue on the body and hackle. Of course, color remains a flexible variant for any pattern, depending upon the particular creatures inhabiting the local waters. A tail on either pattern is more for esthetics than for scientific verity.

The best solution is to study the nymph forms in a particular water and custom design a pattern to suit that form. The most important elements to emulate are color, size and shape. The finer details such as eyes, cilia and wing cases are secondary considerations. One of the more important details is the legs. The legs must pump in the water; therefore, supple hackle fibers are required for the proper illusion.

In the dragonfly nymph's transformation from beast to beauty, a slow and subtle process, there is a certain dignity, fraught with utility, which defies its disgusting, subaquatic costume. It is a monster which I welcome in the dark solvent of my dreams.

Carey Special (dragonfly nymph, impressionistic). Pattern by Colonel Carey. Sizes 2-12. This is the old standby of western waters. Whether it is fished shallowly or deeply, it should be retrieved with a basic hand-twist. It is most effective in heavily weeded lakes.

Thread:	Black.
Tail:	Optional; pheasant breast feather fibers.
Body:	Pheasant tail fibers, tightly wound onto the shank—or green, black or brown chenille, fur or peacock herl.
Thorax:	Continuation of body.
Hackle:	Pheasant flank hackle or mallard breast hackle.

Mongrel (dark dragonfly nymphs, expressionistic). Pattern by Donald Roberts. Sizes 1-12, weighted. Specifically designed for use in the dark waters of many lowland lakes. Incidentally, this is a rewarding pattern for river angling.

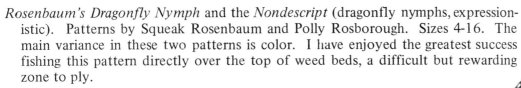

Thread:	Black.
Tail:	None.
Body:	Black seal fur, dubbed and trimmed.
Rib:	Heavy copper wire.
Thorax:	Continuation of body.
Hackle:	One black hackle and one furnace, several turns.

Rosenbaum's Dragonfly Nymph and the *Nondescript* (dragonfly nymphs, expressionistic). Patterns by Squeak Rosenbaum and Polly Rosborough. Sizes 4-16. The main variance in these two patterns is color. I have enjoyed the greatest success fishing this pattern directly over the top of weed beds, a difficult but rewarding zone to ply.

Thread:	Brown or black.
Tail:	Optional; brown marabou or two furnace hackle tips, tied short.
Body:	Colors—dark brown, light brown, tan, dark green, gray or muted yellow; burlap, fur, yarn or wool.
Thorax:	Continuation of body, considerably larger than body.
Hackle:	Brown hen hackle or furnace hackle, several turns from tail to head, trimmed on the tail portion and on the top and bottom of thorax.

Purple Phantom (dragonfly nymph, expressionistic). Pattern by Donald Roberts. Sizes 2-12, long shank, weighted. This pattern is generally fished right on the bottom of well silted lakes. It should be retrieved as slowly as the fisherman can endure.

Thread:	Black.
Tail:	Peacock sword herl.
Body:	Gray muskrat, dubbed and trimmed, purple marabou dubbed over muskrat fur.
Rib:	Several turns of peacock herl and silver wire.
Thorax:	Two strands of black ostrich herl.
Underhackle:	Optional; short, stiff furnace hackle.
Hackle:	Pheasant rump feather, amber or ginger sheen.

Doll's Hair (dragonfly nymph, expressionistic). Pattern by David Tolman. Sizes 2-16. This fly is tied using the kind of acrylic deep pile that is used for making doll's hair. That is as far as make believe goes. This pattern, as simple as it is, qualifies as the single most mercenary nymph I have ever used.

Thread:	Black.
Tail:	None.
Body:	Brown acrylic, dubbed and trimmed in the shape of a football.
Thorax:	Same as body, but smaller.
Hackle:	Brown teal flank or grouse flank feather, two turns between the head and the body.

Jindabyne Special (dragonfly nymph, expressionistic). Originator of pattern unknown. Sizes 2-12. I brought this fly back from Australia, where I purchased it to be used in Lake Jindabyne, New South Wales. I have since used it in rivers and lakes throughout the West. It is indispensable as a night pattern.

Thread:	Black.
Tail:	Optional; black or red wool tuft.
Body:	Black wool or black seal fur.
Thorax:	Continuation of body.
Wing:	One black, one royal blue (dyed) mallard flank feather, tied flat over body.
Hackle:	Orange or crimson hen hackle, tied back to follow contour of body.

THE AUTHOR'S FAVORITE STILL WATER FLIES:

Giant Crayfish

Seaweed's Crawdad

Golden Girl

Cream Caddis   Timberline   Ghost Bug   Zug Bug   Heather Nymph

Chrome Bug Green   Chrome Bug Maroon   Aquabug   Kaufmann's Emergent   Unkempt

Little Gray Caddis   Trueblood Shrimp   Timberline Emerger   Public Enemy No. 1   Damselfly Nymph

Black Collar   Greenhead   Purple Phantom   Black and White   Jindabyne Special

Lakestone Green   Carey Special   Rosenbaum's Dragon   Doll's Hair

Moose Mane   Giant Waterbug   Mongrel   Lakestone Red

Top: A British Columbia wilderness cutthroat lake. Bottom: A mountain lake mirrored by snow. — Photos by Byron Nance

Top: Spawning three-pound brook trout before release. Bottom: Stillness of a desert reservoir. — Photos by Diana Roberts

Top: Morning on an alpine lake. Bottom: Sunset on a desert lake. — Photos by Diana Roberts

Chapter VII

Profiles: A Line on Lakes

eferring to lake waters as "still" is largely relative. There is always some kind of current, some tiny turbulence, some commotion, no matter how subtle or imperceptible. The layers of the lake migrate, the molecules bounce with conductive energy, streams flow in and out like seasonal arteries, and the sky argues, wrangles, irritates the lake's tranquil complexion and serene countenance.

Despite the atmospheric disturbance, lake water remains a stickier substance than that of rivers. The relative inertia of lake water allows the fish a medium for morbid perusal; no imitation escapes leisurely inspection. In rivers the fly is borne by the trout in the grip of the current; the fly is a fleeting form, a nearly subliminal enticement. In lakes you must create your own current, your own illusions. The lake fisherman becomes animator and artist, a man with an act.

The West is abundant with waters where a man can practice his act, perfect his performance, begin to believe his own magic. Although this is not an exhaustive study (such an endeavor would require volumes), I do try to present fleeting profiles of various lakes which are representative. Hopefully these experiential accounts will suggest the manner and the mode from which productive generalities are generated.

Lowland Lakes

West Medical Lake: A Fine Madness   *Spokane County, Washington*

During the '76 Presidential campaign, President Ford made a brief stopover in Spokane. The politics were perfunctory, and protocol was slashed to a bare minimum as Ford casually dismissed the affairs of state to ask his surprised hosts to take him fishing.

West Medical, which is approximately a half hour from Spokane by limousine, was the lake chosen to entertain the President. It is a worthy, although strange, body of water, as rewarding to the common man as to heads of state...not to mention the wards of the bordering Mental Hospital.

West Medical is a small, spring-fed lake in deceptively barren terrain, a region of grasslands, scrub pine and wheat fields. It is a consistently temperate lake well suited to encourage the nitrogen-oxygen exchange of plant and animal, each generated on the other's waste. The dark, volcanic soil obscures the limpid waters and supplies rich nutrients to plants which flourish over the entire bottom of this shallow lake. The resulting insect and crustacean population supports and nourishes an enormous concentration of spirited trout. Considering West Medical's unfortunate location in the virtual backyard of an urban center, its success seems to defy simple logic. Yet, when one examines the almost perfect balance of soil, water, plant and animal life, the puzzle becomes less perplexing.

The only problem with West Medical is its popularity. On the opening day of fishing season you can literally walk across the lake without touching the water and wonder amidst the snarl of boats and hardware and fat ladies in Bermuda shorts, "just who is crazy?" The aberrants on the other side of the gray cyclone fence which skirts the area?...or the deranged mob of sportsmen fighting to slip the bonds of social consequence?

I would not recommend that anyone with tranquil motives approach the lake until the opening season mania has subsided. But in May, especially on an obscure week day, West Medical becomes a deep nymph fisherman's laboratory. This lake is a classic dragonfly breeding ground.

The last time I fished West Medical was on a woeful Wednesday in early May. The weather had turned disagreeable; the sky, a bomb-metal gray, was shoved across the landscape by a belligerent wind laced with icy shrapnel, the kind of day which should be banned by the Geneva Convention. I had the lake to myself and a rented rowboat which veered to the left and came equipped with a rusty bilge can. As I dug into the water with splintered oars, always opposing the wind, stopping to bail out some of the lake, feeling the rain dart against my neck, I looked across the weather-disputed landscape at the government impoundment, the web of cyclone fence trimmed with stark strands of barbed wire. Somewhere, probably confined to distant quarters, were the patients, people trapped in the matrix of their own sprung reality. In the meantime I struggled with my own brand of lunacy.

I had one rod rigged with a floating line, with a petite damselfly nymph dangling on a long leader. The rod tip hung over the transom with the nymph skipping on the water three feet behind the boat. I kept this outfit prepared in the case of a surface feed. With the other rod I worked out 50 to 60 feet of high density line, loaded with a short leader and a stout dragonfly nymph. Using the drift of the boat, I eased out another 30 feet of line. Then I held the boat in check against the wind while the line draped itself through the dark interior of the lake. After approximately one minute I allowed the boat to start creeping across the lake, resisting the headstrong wind with slowly treading oars. I scissored the rod between my legs, scanned the cyclone fence, and considered the Freudian implications of this strange endeavor.

After drifting only a few feet the rod bowed sharply and slammed against my shin bone. A large rainbow went into an airborne tantrum so far to the side of the boat that the event seemed unattached to the struggle ensuing in the boat. As I pumped in the line in a furious attempt to make a direct connection, to hotline the rod to the fish, a swirl engulfed the other carelessly trailing fly. The rod tipped up sharply, and I lunged at it as it slid across the transom. I had a rod in each hand with two heavy fish wrenching their guts out in the wind and rain-flecked water.

The appropriate way to agitate a lake.

51

The futility of the situation created in me a sense of rational detachment. The boat shot over the lake aimlessly, though always veering dependably to the left. I stood in the rain, watching the cyclone fence, gripping two pulsating rods. I wondered, with ambivalence, on which side of the fence a chronic was most likely to be found.

With more a sense of relief than despair the damselfly ripped free of the leader as a disgruntled trout wore it into the depths, a decoration on the occasion of freedom. I put the other fish to task, finally winning the privilege to decide its fate.

As long as the nymph is kept slowly inching its way through the bottom-bound weeds or perhaps even skating on the ill tempered surface, the odd confines of West Medical will give up handsome fish. On a mean day, adrift on such waters, one does not question the spurious genetics of the nymph fisherman.

Surely his case is acute.

Lake Chelan: Born of Beasts   *Chelan County, Washington*

Lake Chelan is a clear, deep body of water, where you can look right down almost into the heart of the earth. It is a lake which covers the world's viscera like an expanded, sun-blistered membrane. It is a gigantic, organic-shaped lake in the tradition of Klamath in Oregon, Pend Oreille in Idaho, Flathead in Montana, and Almanor in California. Chelan's sheer size is perplexing, reproachful, somewhat threatening.

Lake Chelan is 55 miles long, no more than 1½ miles wide in any spot, and over 1,600 feet deep in many places. It is a place of legends, of monsters, and least of all, of mortal man.

According to the grandson of Chief Wapato of the Chelan tribe, a monster came into the country, which was then a great broad plain. The monster ate the elk, deer, bear and all other animals. The Great Spirit heard the prayers of the starving people and killed the monster. Life returned to normal for many years, and the people prospered. Then the monster mysteriously reappeared, this time with an even larger appetite. The people once again implored the Great Spirit to rid them of the monster. The Great Spirit felt sympathy for the people and killed the monster again. After many more years the monster came back to life and returned to ravage the land. The Great Spirit became annoyed and angered. He came down to relieve the desperate people of the persistent monster for the last time. He slaughtered the monster, then struck the earth with a huge stone knife. A cloud rose and covered the landscape. When the cloud fled, the people saw enormous mountains and long canyons. The Great Spirit threw the monster's body into the bottom of this deep, long gorge, then covered it with water.

The monster never came again, but its tail refused to die. Sometimes even yet it thrashes around and causes big waves on the surface of the lake. The Indians avoid the monster's watery grave. No one has ever found the very bottom.

Lake Chelan is a blue, frosty plain where the fish seem as scarce as wandering antelope; yet they are plentiful in the preferred regions, the attractive enclaves where the fish herd. The cutthroat and rainbow roam the food shelf, the outer rim of the lake, and they congregate at the mouths of Chelan's countless feeder streams. You must anticipate them...be there when they materialize.

In the early summer through fall the water is so clear that the trout move only when you blink. Casts must be graceful, precise. Cast close to the irregular shoreline where a stream enters and dissipates into the cosmic medium of still water. The trout are usually there, suspended in the single frame of a celluloid moment. A nymph that struggles or thrashes into the trout's screen presses an instinctual switch, the circuitry crackles, and the trout flashes forward to intercept the larva, to foreshorten their mutual destiny.

52

If there is evidence of mayflies, a Timberline or Timberline Emerger often proves effective. In the event that no mayflies are visible, a caddis pattern is a reliable constant. Mayflies are most abundant in the Chelan country until about mid-June. Caddisflies emerge sporadically during the entire season.

I have found the single most effective method for searching the stream mouths and lake inlets to be the Leisenring Lift. This technique was developed by James Leisenring to be used in rivers. If executed properly, this method imitates most faithfully an emerging nymph, a life cycle phenomena not restricted to moving water and therefore as useful on lakes as streams.

Employ a long leader and a floating line. Cast the fly into a trout lie, but never right over the fish. Allow the line reverberations to subside and the weighted nymph to sink a few feet. Then lift the rod upward in one smooth motion. Pull the bow out of the line as you lift. The illusion created is of the nymph rushing to the surface, anxious to divorce the underwater world for the brief, consuming interlude of adulthood. Normally wary trout are struck with serious disorders of judgment when presented with the compelling image of a meal levitating into their sights.

Sometimes the takes are so swift and stealthy that the jaded trout is already a fleeting shadow before you can detect the slightest aberration in the line. Watch for a flutter of light, a nervous tic in the line, the glint of the sun twisting off the fish like the edge of a submerged knife. Set the hook even if you only suspect...do not expect anything in particular, especially consistency. The next fish may attempt to rip the knobs off your finger tips.

Like the fish in Lake Chelan, avoid the dark, morbid abysses. While staring down into aqua-canyons, the monster of myths may stir, its tail spasmodic with unrequited wrath. It may manufacture images in the mind's eye, fresh and squirming, a product of man's contemplation of the dreaded, incomprehensible deep.

Davis Lake: Stalk Still Waters   *Deschutes County, Oregon*

The square, copper tail rose monolithically out of the water and wavered unnervingly, the gesture of a contented rainbow, head down, sucking the meat from the soup of the day. My mind rapidly calculated the size of the animal attached to the sunlit tail, a flare of impassioned figures, the buzzing of a disturbed Ahab. I credited myself with maintaining reasonable calm, a solid suppression of the glands.

Trout usually establish feeding routines, moving parallel to the shoreline in elliptical patterns as if assigned stations. This trout was oblivious to drill; its sheer size enforced disorder. It roamed randomly, grazing through a caddis nymph souffle. I had no idea where he would surface next, so I had to contend with unresolved tension. An impetuous cast at the wrong moment would certainly create more than just alpha-waves. It could cause the brutish prize to sound into oblivion.

While I waited for the next sign, I tied on a No. 6 Unkempt, caddis pattern. With the surplus of larvae in the water I reasoned that an extravagant-sized offering would be conspicuous by its deformity. An enormous dorsal fin silently sliced the surface. I gauged its speed and direction of movement.

My cast straightened out over the water, then dropped weightlessly, as if narrowly slotted by destiny to fit only this space. The mutant nymph wavered through the trout's window like the most blatant of passing billboards. The near perfection of my presentation impressed me immensely; the trout, however, disregarded the egotistical assumption and callously turned, snubbing the nymph with a flick of his tail. I ripped my cast off the water like a deranged general tearing the stripes off a cowardly soldier and lurched through another cast. An ill timed and spasmodic wad of line honored my energy. Miraculously the line unraveled in mid-air and sent the fly plummeting like a crippled Boeing 747. The nymph opened a crater in the water within inches of the languid form. I expected the silver animal to disappear in sparks of sunlight. Instead the trout bent backward like a dog attempting to slash at a flea and calmly assaulted the fly. I obliged the creature's perverse judgment and lifted the rod. The trout, momentarily disillusioned but not disheartened by this flimsy shackle, surged directly toward me, then kicked its entire length sideways into the air, assigning itself a lofty position above me. The trout seemed to hover there, unnaturally defying the laws of physical science. It eyed me, a hard, frank, lidless stare, an expressionless glare which previewed escape. I followed its descent with the rod, feeling its life jolt in my arm sockets.

Small trout tingle your fingers, but the big ones pull right through your entire bone structure, telegraphing dumb panic. The fisherman is at once fused with the energy of struggle but also weakened by a chaos of nerves. And if fish were not silent creatures? If they could scream, whimper and grunt anthropomorphically? It is almost certain their baffled rage would do little to amuse all but the most vicious species of man. Vowelless struggles save us from sentimental affliction.

The great, aged trout sounded toward a dark, submarine stage, where it paused to shake its head, an emphatic "no". The leader finally submitted; a microscopic lesion terminated the struggle. The trout exited into a purple curtain of water. No second act. No encores.

Even though I had posed no real threat to the trout's fate, just hooking such a creature is gratifying. I reeled in, sans ceremony, a length of backing violated all too seldom. I have heard many fishermen on similar occasions swear defiantly. I prefer to reflect on what was, rather than on what might have been. The privilege of wrath is too often sorely abused.

The tree-lined shores of Davis Lake have absorbed the ranting and raving of all too many jilted monster hunters.

Davis Lake is a place where you can find all classes of fish and fishermen. It is one of the only easily accessible lakes where trophy fish are not uncommon, appearing as suddenly as apparitions in the unflawed shallows. Davis offers a diversity of holding water ranging from crumbling basalt edifices to wide sunlit shallows and rich, verdant weed beds.

The entire lake is closed to angling from motor propelled craft, and much of the lake is reserved for fly-only angling. Despite this regard for quality and tranquillity, I have never explored Davis without observing trollers and numerous so-called sportsmen callously ignoring the regulations. Fortunately, the majority of anglers visiting Davis are conscientious and thoughtful, strengthening the fraternity of fishermen honor-bound to the quality concept.

Davis Lake hosts a variety of larvae, which accommodates diverse methods and approaches. If there is no evidence of emerging mayflies or caddisflies, a dragonfly nymph or an ambiguous water bug pattern slithered along the contours of the food shelf, or over weed beds, or along the edges of basalt rubble will almost certainly provoke an assault. Carey Specials, Ghost Bugs and Lakestone nymphs serve well throughout the season as searcher patterns.

Experiment. Probe. Create illusions which more than ape reality. Davis Lake is the raw material of transcendence.

Alpine Lakes

Chopaka Lake: Peripheral Vision   *Okanogan County, Washington*
Alpine lakes like Chopaka are relatively untroubled by man's tampering. Lack of easy access, intemperate and unpredictable weather, and primitive facilities discourage the madding crowd. Thank God that coke machines, flush toilets and power boats are limited to malignant resorts on paved-access lakes.

The last couple of miles of road into Chopaka Lake are of a stubborn tilt. It is a resistant incline and geologic barrier to Winnebagos, cabin cruisers and luxurious motel rooms on wheels. Chopaka is one of the few places left where camping is still largely an outdoor activity.

Chopaka Lake lies along the lower anatomy of the Cascades, like a silver coin lost on a blue stair of rock. Pine and fir trees of noble stature maintain scattered vigil over the slopes, acting as sky hooks set for the clouds. The lake lies at the cloud line, where barometric conditions are unstable, whimsical, moody. The winds are spontaneous and argumentative. It often rains in the sunlight, and schizoid snowstorms regularly mock the early summer. Morning mists unfurl humorlessly over the lake like airy gauze, to simmer and finally dissolve in the consuming air. The stolid silence of the mountain-scape is the essence of sudden acquittal from urban concerns.

In keeping with the integrity of the scenario, Chopaka is a fly only, barbless hook water. There is a five-fish limit, although few fishermen keep as many rainbow and cutthroat as they are allowed.

The rainbows prowl predaciously, weaving through the weed channels and along the shallow shelves, while cutthroat flash like scattered silverware in the procelain light. Chopaka Lake rainbows are fired along the spine with a dark blue, like the cool traces of a welder's seam, and they are as heavy as metal slabs warming in their captor's hands. The cutthroat are sleek and uniform, machined from nature with precise redundancy, tatooed on the throat, a sublime labeling.

Chopaka Lake is so transparent, so revealing that it is unnerving. Fishing in such virtuous water is as much like marriage as it is not. First you must attract your quarry with your own form, before you impale it on your hook. There is no murk to obscure the design; each cast stands naked. Fortunately, the marriage metaphor extends itself; after all, fish are no less gullible than infatuated lovers. A studied presentation can induce irrational proposals. In the eagerness for consumption the fish's vision becomes blurred, obvious flaws are ignored, and appetite supersedes judgment.

As in all alpine lakes, the shoreline around Chopaka is consistently attractive to larger fish. While other fishermen are maneuvering their craft over water haystacks searching for the proverbial needle, I am usually flanking the shoreline, creeping on hands and knees with the patience of a cat, although little of the malicious indifference. The importance of the edging effect cannot be too strongly stressed.

On one warm afternoon in early June, with the clouds as jumbled and mellow in the bleached sky as scrambled eggs on china, I crawled along a rockslide at the west end of Chopaka and examined the water with a polaroid-shrouded eye. Chopaka was still and secretive, but as I sat motionless and watched the debris sloping into the clear water I noticed cased caddisflies invading the rock projections like miniature masonry. I tied on a No. 6 Moose Mane and dropped the sinking line over the landslide of rock. Then I retrieved the line with a painfully slow hand-twist intended to emulate the caddisfly's bellying along in their temporary housing. The large trout, which were hunkered between boulders like moray eels, took the offering with slow and deliberate menace, a style of strike calculated to be confused with snags, of which there were many. Although this type of fishing is frustrating, sometimes infuriating, its effectiveness can hardly be disputed.

I lost a half dozen flies that afternoon and caught two trout big enough to make my wrists ache. For fish of that caliber no sacrifice justifies pause; all resulting aches are sweet indeed.

That evening the rockslide became fickle. It continued to inflict a high rate of mortality on my motley legion of flies, but gave up no fish in return. I admitted defeat and continued to follow the shoreline on its irregular route until it dissipated into a vague and sprawling marsh where red willows sagged sullenly and the reeds bristled in clumps. As is common on alpine lakes, even during the blustery days, the evening air became comatose. Despite the absolute stillness, the reeds stirred softly, jostled by trespassing fish. The trout were rummaging through the stalks, searching for damselflies and dragonflies which latch onto the submerged reeds, securing a position for the final stages of larval adolescence.

I eased out to the edge of the reeds until the silt bubbled up phlegmatically at chest level on my waders. I cast into the open water parallel to the reeds, using a No. 8 Black Collar, on a floating line and a long leader. I allowed the fly to sink only seconds, then retrieved the fly in irregular time, a staccato pulse, the jazz beat rhythm. The rainbows invariably took the nymph on the downbeat as it sank motionless, stunned in space. Each trout came slashing from the side, barging through the reeds, causing a swelling in my knuckles and my adrenalin glands to slosh drunkenly.

One particularly incorrigible Chopaka specimen charged my fly in a manner of ambush that I have never seen before or since. That fish rammed clear of the reeds, passed by the fly on a deranged course, circled back in a swirl that left a suckhole twirling in the moonlight, then swooped upward, clearing the water, and flamboyantly, if not blindly, bounced the fly off its nose like a seal doing tricks.

Somewhere in that Cascade tarn there is a trout which unstrings fishermen like ruptured violins.

Yellowstone Lake: Cook's Choice   *Yellowstone Park, Montana*

Yellowstone Lake, pressing skyward at 7,733 feet, is not only one of the highest and largest alpine lakes in the world, but it also yields more native cutthroat trout than any other lake on this planet. Approximately three million people a year drive by the lake; fortunately, most of these people comment on its beauty and keep on caravaning. Even though only a fraction of the visitors to the park actually fish the lake, it is pressured by thousands of anglers during its three-month season.

Most of the fishermen congregate at favored locations along parts of the north and west side of Yellowstone Lake. For every mile that is heavily stomped there is three miles of virtually untouched water. All of one side of Yellowstone Lake's 20-mile length is inaccessible except by boat.

Fishing Bridge, located where Yellowstone River pours out of the lake, is in itself a spectator phenomena. Cutthroat, none under a foot long, throng in almost military order under the bridge in the newborn current. Every form of flake and pseudo-fisherman clusters above, a chaotic assemblage. The fish, having seen it all, are indifferent and immune to every kind of bait or lure ever hurled, tossed, plunked or dunked. Fishing Bridge is a zoo where angling is reduced to charades, the pursuer and the pursued each trying to guess what the other is doing, both in full view, but even more abstracted and farther removed from reality by the candid clarity of the intervening space. It is a place well suited to strict avoidance. But if you ever do trespass on such insanity, for God's sake roll up your car windows while crossing the bridge, unless you picture yourself, in your darkest subconscious, firmly ensnared at the serious end of a bent rod and a blazing Zebco. Although, I have never seen a fish caught at Fishing Bridge, I have witnessed countless human encounters worthy of features in psychological journals.

I worked at Lake Hotel for two seasons and spent much of that time fishing that area directly in front of the hotel. As is often the case, the least likely area for miles around contained a startling population of large fish. Perhaps Fishing Bridge attracted all of the crazies. That left only me to haunt the lonely shores of the derelict Lake Hotel, a DiJon mustard yellow roadhouse hulking in the breathless pines.

Unless you plan on going out in a boat, do not pass up the opportunity to fish

during stormy, wind thrashed days. As the poet Richard Grafton said in 1569, "They may the better fish in the water when it is troubled."

At Yellowstone Lake summer storms are common, replete with torrential rains, hail, and lightning that spits blue splinters. These atmospheric tantrums lash across the lake, churning the water darkly and transforming the shoreline into a ragged, snarling jaw, the rocks bared against the purple fulgurous sky like foam-flecked teeth. On numerous occasions I have violated the lonely sanctity and somewhat false bravado of the summer tempests to dare the lightning with my rod, to aggravate fate with my presence. On many such forays into the occluded breach I have been rewarded with equally foolhardy trout. One particular occasion stands out in my mind because of the sudden appearance of the cook.

Gale force winds were assaulting the beach head on, and I had little choice, short of hiking a hundred miles through wilderness to get to the other side, but to oppose the wind with my casts. It had little effect on my optimism because I needed to cast only about 30 feet to reach a pile of rocks and old dock pilings where I knew several obese cutthroat held territorial dominance. I used a size 6 Stonefly nymph on a floating line and a short, stout leader. I cast over the debris, where the storm-lashed water ground against dissolving boulders. No finesse. I simply pumped against the wind, forcing the cast defiantly into the roiled water which boiled above the forgotten dock and stone sentinels.

I caught and released several trout, each one further immunizing my skin to the grit of driven rain, but the last fish was different. As it billowed in the half-light, I recognized immediately its excess of flesh and power. I felt it right through to my boots; it generated a heat which obliterated all acknowledgment of the storm, of the lightning which fizzed and snapped like spit on a wood stove. I was immersed in the dull roar of submerged noises, like sinking into the froth of a crowded swimming pool.

I danced with that fish. It led...I followed, struggling with the pain of fun. An odd couple, strung together like strangers at an alien dance hall.

Suddenly the cook appeared...shouting at my back, transforming the metaphor. He was the man on the periphery of battle, having placed his bet, now bellowing instructions to his adopted fighter.

"Tighten up! Pull his head around. Easy now. He's running. Let him go. Give him his head. Now put it to him. He's tiring...My God, look at that fish jump!"

The cook still had his starched whites on; the rain beaded on his black oxfords. Traces of the lunch hour onslaught were streaked down his shirt, yellow divots of mayonnaise, moist speckles of grease, and dried sienna ketchup. The cook coached, chided, sympathized.

After a series of shorter and shorter desperate runs the fish surfaced, listing with fatigue. I kept the line strung to E sharp and backed up the bank. The animal seemed resigned to the situation until it passed over the blackened, rotted pilings and corroded iron plates, the place where old tour boats used to ram to full-stop at the dock.

The cook was sidestepping, shuffling, giggling with unnatural glee. He could barely resist grabbing the line and hand-lining the trout directly into his lap. The fish had yet to entirely forsake its freedom; it seized its only opportunity and plummeted under a stray iron plate which was wedged into some rocks in about three feet of water. The cook stumbled back, horrified and dumbstruck. I felt the leader angle sharply against the ragged edge of iron. I could not increase the pressure without cutting the line. It would only be moments before the trout shook its head and frayed the leader.

The cook moved instinctively, as if in a trance. He waded in, polished oxfords and all, visibly drawing an anguished breath as the 47° water slurped at his belt. He

58

clenched his fists and delivered a series of slow-motion kicks into the groin of the submerged iron bunker. The trout spurted from the enclave and spent the remainder of its energy in one throbbing run.

I carefully unhooked the 22-inch cutthroat and laid it in the cook's cradled arms. It had been my fight, but it was his fish.

Jewel Lake: Mountain Gem   *British Columbia, Canada*

Jewel Lake was a last ditch effort, a discovery resulting from desperation. The rain had been unrelenting, and I had persisted in fishing the famous Williams Lake region, despite the protestations from my wife, who sat in the car and glumly read gothic romances for three days. I continued to maintain that I was not a fair weather fisherman, that the fish were there, that if they were there they had to be feeding. Three days of religious effort proved only the first premise to be true. The latter two remained to be seen.

Did I detect superior glances from my wife as I sullenly traversed the soggy British Columbia landscape on our way home? A few miles before reaching the border of northeastern Washington, I saw a sign pointing north toward a casual, satin-green ridge...Jewel Lake in small black letters. We had two days of vacation left and bacon in the ice chest and enough potato chips to feed a Panzer division of chipmunks.

Jewel Lake—the name was promising. I turned impulsively. About four miles up the ridge in an anonymous range of low, worn mountains, I looked in the rearview mirror and saw an expanding trail of dust. Dust? The first time dust had ever suggested a good omen. We were driving into a paradise hidden from the overlords of rain.

We secured a cabin for $4.00 a night and our choice of leaky row boats for $2.00 a day. The lake was deserted as the clouds tumbled by to drown vacations in other places. Most astounding of all—the lake was equal to its name. Jewel Lake was an oval sapphire glistening in the junction of two wooded ridges. It was a lake reminiscent of a thousand other alpine lakes which enrich the Rockies, the Cascades, the Blues and every wildcat ridge, geologic extrusion and scab batholith in the West. But it was not until we were out in the lake that the comparisons became specific.

The shores were lined with slash. Stumps, spiked logs and assorted debris cluttered the small, irregular bays. The lake's unflawed transluscence revealed thickets of channeled and cavernous emerald green weed beds. I was reminded of Browns Lake in the Skookum country, of Strawberry Lake in the Blue Mountains, of Perregrine in the Cascades, and countless others. All of these lakes possess a common, eerie and ominous demeanor. There is the constant suggestion of creatures hidden in their submerged and twisted forms. While peering down in the ever-darkening decline it is easy to imagine hideous monsters and vermiculous giants. All of these lakes have spawned Indian legends, but most of the myths have been lost in the rapid dissolve of the indigenous Indian cultures.

Fish Lake near Mt. Adams is a distant twin of Jewel Lake. It is one of those lakes worthy and deserving of mystical tales. In its water is the aura of a lost culture. The water is so clear that trout can be seen darting in and out of the holes which riddle the bottom. The Klickitat believed that the holes were entry ways of spirits and dragons. They were forbidden to fish in the lake, under penalty of death. They feared they would anger the dragon, which would fly about causing havoc and famine.

Given the superstitious background of such lakes, perhaps we brazen and hard-hearted fishermen should change techniques. What creatures could we lure into the glare of reality with the appropriate offerings? Perhaps we should troll with whole, freshly-slaughtered gamecocks or beheaded peacocks or wet flies tied from unicorn tails and sprinkled with powdered rhinocerous horn.

Such thoughts passed through my mind as I stared into Jewel Lake, scanning its morbid maze of sunken trees and weed beds. My wife paused in her privileged task, raised the dripping oars, leaned her chin on the crossed handles, and fixed me with her gaze as if to inquire, "Where have you been?" The legends lost their fire as I snapped back to reality. It didn't matter anyway; the legends of Jewel Lake had been eradicated long ago, erased obliquely by the manifestations of civilization. I looked back into the interior of the lake, beyond the superficial beauty, and was reassured. Despite the deplorable absence of ancient myth, there is, when you peer into the abyss, the savage makings of untold tales.

I settled for the modest hauntings of trout as my wife resumed her nautical exercises. I searched the area for surface activity, but the lake was as untroubled by feeding fish as bottled water. I fastened a sinking line to my rod, added a foot of four-pound tippet to the eight-foot leader and tied on a size 8 Purple Phantom dragonfly nymph pattern. I instructed my wife to hover over the channels in the weed beds while I worked out line. I manipulated the nymph, which was visible at all times, to a depth of about 20 feet and retrieved across the bottom of the channel, moving it slowly and imparting a pulsating effect with the rod tip.

A small-headed, thick-bodied rainbow bolted from cover to batter the fly. I was compelled to act energetically but not impulsively as the stung fish struggled for the cover available on every flank. I lost many more Jewel Lake trout than I confused and bullied into capture.

As evening neared I ignored my wife's amorous glances and the suggestions of cabin sport (there are priorities) to switch to a floating line and the strongly positive-negative, high contrast Black and White pattern. My wife dutifully maintained the helm; humoring my obsession, she rowed us into the shallows where the weeds curled and rolled just below the surface. I probed the pockets, allowing the fly to sink down two or three feet, then reversing it with a Leisenring Lift. The strikes were abrupt, yet smooth, the practiced art of waterbound kleptomaniacs. In all but the rarest cases the trout also stole their freedom, fleeing back into their weedy ghettos.

When it became so dark that the hills, trees and water melted into one sauce, I was forced to stop. The realm of darkness returned the lake, that precious gem, to its rightful owners, the inhabitants of legends...the monsters.

Desert Lakes

Higgins Reservoir: A Lake Without Signs   *Baker County, Oregon*

Higgins Reservoir nestles among the rimrocks about eight miles north of the sub-compact town of Unity in eastern Oregon. There are no signs, but if you turn left at the garbage dump on the east side of town and stay on the road which has the deepest ruts you will get there eventually. If you prefer more specific directions, stop at the Waterhole Tavern in Unity and inquire; the proprietor can describe every rock and chuckhole for miles around. While you are there, invest in one of their two-handed hamburgers and a milkshake, which must be excavated with a spoon. In the event you do get lost, such a repast will guarantee survival for several days.

Do not attempt to go into Higgins if it has been raining. If it starts to rain seriously while you are there, break camp immediately. The clay dry-washes which blot the open range are instant swamps waiting to happen. I have seen the most formidable four-wheel drive rigs which have ever churned over the earth mired up to their sun visors in the yellow-ochre, desert paste, looking as pathetic as dinosaurs slowly expiring in custard.

There are very few trees around Higgins. The few willows which have brashly resisted the harsh terrain provide favored locales for the much unloved but never ignored rattlesnake. If you prefer cool forests of whispering pine, Higgins is not for you. It is more a lake for those leathery souls whose aversion to humanity and fondness for introspection leads them into landscapes of the most anti-romantic inclination. The desert is so unpleasant, so unmolded to social comforts, that it is pleasant.

At Higgins there is no level camping area. The access is limited and at best, rough. There is an abundance of rattlesnakes. There is very little shade and no fresh water. Obviously, there is no dock, no launching ramp, no toilets, no electricity, and no nearby phone. The burrs are tenacious; the rocks are jagged; the wind is perverse; and the sun is tortuously constant. In short, Higgins is an excellent area for the solitary pursuit of large trout. It is a place which invites total, sentient darkness at night and a sun that roars by day. Moderation is a totally alien concept to the desert landscape.

Higgins Reservoir is about a mile long and a quarter of a mile wide. It is fed by a small stream and by submerged, oozing springs. The highly alkaline water is conducive to heavy weed growth, which in turn supports a concentration of scuds, crawfish, damsel and dragonflies. The ample insect link in the food chain contributes to a growth rate for rainbows which exceeds one inch per month. During the high cycle years a fish below two pounds is a rare specimen to be regarded with mute curiosity.

The bottom of the reservoir is carpeted bank to bank with a deep-pile shag of weeds, which limits for the most part the viable fishing water to the epilimnion, or top layer. The large trout in Higgins are the most vulnerable in the evening, when they prowl the weeded shallows. In the gray veil of evening their gluttony is almost indiscriminate, although a large, dark-bodied dragonfly nymph is particularly favored. Other productive patterns include the Chrome Bug, Seaweed's Crawdad, Black Collar, and Jindabyne Special.

The most productive method is to drift the weed beds, working the nymph through the channels and pockets. A canoe or an inflatable raft is especially useful for this purpose. In the near darkness a white, floating line best telegraphs any sign of a take. Ironically, large trout engulf the fly with the most delicate of manners. It cannot be stressed too often that the least movement of the line must be addressed with an immediate reaction. The rod should be lifted smoothly, not jerked, and the line hauled tight in the same fluid action. The hook should be set, not plowed, into the fish's jaw.

In the subdued light it is possible to get by with an inordinately heavy leader, although the tippet must be light enough not to impair the action of the nymph. At least six-pound test is necessary to halt determined trout short of assured escape in the shrouds of weed. If a resolute fish is allowed even a moment of sanctuary in its watery briar patch, the game is over, resulting in one hit (the trout's), one run (the trout's), and one error (yours).

It is the desert night which is a final reward for a day of angling. There is no other place where the canopy of the universe is laid out in such terrifying extremes, the simple threat of the continuum, the devastating incomprehensibility of infinity. There is no other place where one's inner ministrations become more articulate, where the heartbeat is louder, where the blood pressure slows to a more auditory gurgle.

Under the focus of a desert night, I see myself as through the opposite end of a telescope. Thus in proper scale, a perspective reduced by reality, I like to wander down to the lake with a flashlight, to throw a beam on the water and set the stage for a world smaller than my own. I like to crush soda crackers in my fist and sprinkle the spotlighted water. Waterstriders, nervous and erratic, hyperactive creatures on hair-thin, spring-steel legs, dart over and grasp the crumbs as soon as they touch the water.

Feeding these whisper-sized insects is not an act of superior philanthropy, nor the whimsy of a human overlord, but the payment of homage to just a few of the creatures which help support my angling habit. The sense of paradox resulting from the introduction of soda crackers into the natural food chain is not even momentarily entertained. In fact, the waterstriders are no less fond of cheese.

Lake Lenice: Lowland High   *Grant County, Washington*

It is not surprising that dramatic fishing should originate in an area with a dramatic geological past. The Columbia drainage system was birthed from fissures in the earth, molten lava expelled from the wounded crust like radiant, clotted blood. These lava dikes dried in an amber, steamy atmosphere, forming swirled heat patterns and puzzling mazes of caked basalt. Some of these continuous lava labyrinths are the size of entire European countries.

Volcanic activity was followed by glacial deterioration. Mountains of accumulated ice began to slowly expire. As the glaciers shrank, they mobilized, etching, scouring and gouging their histories into the earth. A vast flood then swept the entire region, as if to wash the volcanic disorder clear of the landscape and into the boiling Pacific.

Lake Lenice now occupies a cool niche in the basaltic ridges of the Columbia drainage system. Its green surface glosses over the violent past. To call the area barren is relative: to some it would appear as forsaken as a radioactive wasteland; to others the open terrain and broad relief, posed by sky merging with castles of rock, is tantalizing, an open invitation to the spirit.

Lenice nourishes a turmoil of weeds, tangled like kelp in the bays and rock crevices, leaving only gullies and cavities of open water. Nymphs of every description swarm in the vegetation, competing with the crustaceans which dominate the vermiculous vegetation. The Lenice rainbows find these worm-infested salads totally to their liking, a high protein playground for ingestive romps.

Lake Lenice is a quality water of some renown in the Northwest. The current limit allowed each angler is three fish per day over 12 inches. Most fishermen elect to return the trout as an investment in larger fish and a higher challenge. Because of the fly only, barbless hook regulations few fish are killed or maimed. Fly fishing equipment is the only acceptable means for angling, and boats with motors are strictly prohibited. Lake Lenice has a split season dating April 17 to July 4 and October 1 to November 30. Owing to Lenice's fame for large fish, it is one quality water which is strictly regulated and patrolled.

Despite its reputation, Lenice is not an easy place to catch fish. Besides having the right fly the fisherman must also possess a surplus of persistence and boundless energy. In most instances a floating line and a long leader with about a six-pound test tippet is the most useful rig. Many fishermen opt for the long, heavy rods, but much of the essence of the experience is lost while employing bulky levers. For the sake of matching the caliber to the game, I prefer a 7 to 8½-foot rod that takes a five or six weight line.

I have rarely witnessed a hatch of any kind on Lenice, or any other desert lake. The surplus of larva in the water at all times tends to inhibit sporadic and explosive feeds. Although there is a visible feed in the early mornings and evenings, the large fish are generally caught sometime during midday. I am firmly of the opinion that most large fish succumb to an impulse, bursting from cover to slug down an overly tempting morsel. Flies of excessive size, those that defy the limits of nature, are often responsible for larger fish. In a lush environment, abounding with food, exaggeration is the key to attraction. Large fish are sometimes deceived by sheer flamboyance.

At Lenice it is necessary to defy convention, to fish during the "off" hours and to thoroughly comb the byways and pockets in the weed complex. The most effective

patterns are the Purple Phantom, Rosenbaum's Dragon and the Doll's Hair in sizes ranging from an obscene No. 2 to a hefty No. 8. Lenice rainbows are especially wary and line conscious. The fisherman is best advised to maintain a low profile in the boat, to make long casts while staying well back from the water to be probed, and to use at least a nine-foot leader.

The Lenice rainbows do not subscribe to a gentle style; their reluctance to take in no way overshadows the vehemence of the occasional foolish mistake. Almost without exception these pampered rainbows strike with jolting force, seemingly infuriated at the freakish impudence of the trespassing fly.

Inherent in the art of fly fishing is a highly developed sense of consciousness. Accomplishment heightens the ego and increases the rush, the high, the total experience. Arrogance is as manifest in the artist's brushstrokes as in the fisherman's creation of illusion; whether tied on a hook or fastened to a handle, badger hair transforms reality. Artists and fly fishermen must make assumptions about their audience. Their speculations must be confirmed with broad strokes of imagination. Such endeavors are pleasurable; such pleasures are self-centered but no less meaningful.

When Salvador Dali was asked if he took drugs to increase his vision, he replied with scolding clarity, "I am drugs!"

So is Lake Lenice.

Warm Springs Reservoir: Desert Notes   *Harney County, Oregon*
I have heard many old timers speak of Warm Springs as a place to die.

That is a distinct possibility...planned or not, in the reckoning of savage spaces.

Even though this landscape can kill you—or, more precisely, simply let you die—it is one place, perhaps the only place, where the 63.9 million other fishermen have not gathered. The bleak, harsh testimony of desert is immeasurable. There are other cooler, softer, tree-lined spaces where the people attend to the tournament, where the anglers gather to joust for the biggest and the most. At Warm Springs just being there is the highest art.

The lake holds the same mystery as the cradled mass of desert. Each possesses an inscrutable expression. What's under them? What are they hiding?

Releasing a fish back into the water...releasing a breath back into the desert air... it's all the same, as easily misunderstood.

The color of the water changes, creamy green in the morning, polished bronze under the sun, slate gray at last light. The junipers stand back, overlords gesturing from barren hills. Sage, the desert peasantry, crowds the water, durable survivors with limbs as tough as petrified snakes. Despite its station, each tree casts its own shadow.

The lake is molten glass under the fierce sun, a silken kiln with coils aflame on the skullcap of wilderness. It is time to stay low, down around the vapor zone, where hellebore and punchen weave their smell, where the smell is a raft drifting just under the knots of sage, avoiding the wind which rips the smell into little pieces. Find some blue-black shade and stay there until dim time.

If you cannot abide such rigid leisure, take along your sunburn cream and defy the furnace on the water. At the south end of Warm Springs is a dam bellied outward, bent as if pressed by the water. There are no weeds anyplace in the lake, only a sunken gel of microscopic organisms. Dragonfly nymphs slip over the dark pulp of lake bottom, scavenging small fish, other larvae and each other. Trout, like silver wedges, float over the dark chambers, drifting diagonally across the slopes, and devouring the indiscriminate with expressionless grace.

Use a high density line, stout leader and a **Giant Water Bug** or a No. 6 Dragonfly

Nymph. Move your boat so slowly you can feel the vibration in your cheeks. Invent a pattern and stick to it as if commissioned to weave a blanket over the lake. Try a variety of depths until you hook a fish, then adhere to that depth. There is little accident to the posture and habits of the giant 'bows in Warm Springs. Do not expect to catch a fish every hour. These dull animals do not associate; they are strung out all over, but are prone to the same style of living...and dying.

I prefer to wait in the shade, injuring my liver with beer and reading novels or sifting sand through my fist. I prefer to wait on the bank and let the fish come to me. Sometimes they do. In the subdued light when the nighthawk appears, the huge trout invade the bays. First I watch the bullbats, as the nighthawks are rudely called by the desert people.

There is no rush. My gear is poised. In a few minutes the fleshy, pressing palm of heat will curl into a fist and lift drunkenly from the tablelands. The bullbat angles in the sky, making perfect casts, dropping its beak politely, swiftly, accurately into pools of sky, hooking out the flitting insects awakened by darkness.

Then I brush by the clumps of stunted red willow and wonder at the objects glowing unnaturally in the half-light; a pair of torn cotton briefs hanging in the sage, twisted beer cans, a broken bottle, banners of toilet paper, a row of twigs whittled into Y's and stuck into the mud at the water's edge. What spawned this somber display? Some dirty old men? A wild party? A high school field trip?

A pack of coyotes interrupts briefly from some distant mesa. Their cries are broken and desperately comical, the shrieking laughter of startled school girls. It ends as abruptly as it started. The proper heraldry for the lone angler, amused by survival and cool air.

I step into the smooth lake, breaking it open like a package. The smell of water escapes. Some lakes smell like refrigerator ice, some like milk, some like finely chopped lettuce. Warm Springs smells like rain pounding a dusty road.

The cliche slurp of a large rainbow breaks the spell; the residue of man is forgotten. I tear several yards of line off the reel and wait, with the line curling over my boots, for the next appearance. The trout surfaces about 50 feet out, and I sense its direction of movement. I know his path like an empty street and cast ahead of it. The Jindabyne Special flutters onto the water, looking only remotely connected to the white, floating fly line. The nymph sinks into the neighborhood of the rainbow. Then I lift the rod and strip the line in three staccato beats. Pause. There is no startling, raucous take, no lunge of the rod, no boil like an exploded depth charge. The line barely moves, but the change is visible, and no natural phenomena can be blamed, other than...

I lift the rod and pull down on the line at the same instant. Everything changes to a blur; events cannot be separated out; nothing is really clear. It is that moment of automatic, non-thinking, total abandonment to the sensations of struggle that makes flyfishing a universal and attractive enigma.

It doesn't matter whether I caught the trout. A narration of the final bout is irrelevant, if not a squandering of words. It would reduce the final plot to a formula conflict, to competition, to a story requiring resolve.

To the few who trouble the waters at Warm Springs, including those who would go there to die, there is no winning or losing.

The fly fisherman's spire in the sky.

Chapter VIII

Conservation:
Barbed Arguments,
Barbless Hooks

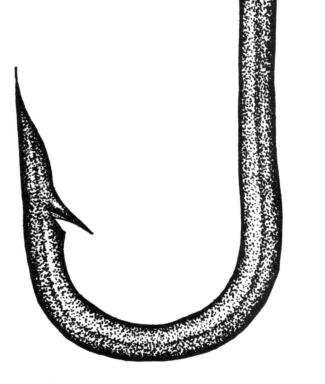

"Piscatorem piscis amare potest?"
—translation: Can the fish love the fisherman?

F ishermen are cruel jewelers, in a sense, prying treasure from the water by unscrupulous fraud. Yet we can partially absolve ourselves from the ruthless implications of the sport simply by returning nature's gem-like creatures to their dumb existence, while their luster is still profound.

The highest goal of fishing isn't catching fish but achieving a kind of protoplasmic consciousness, an almost non-analytical, symbiotic relationship with nature.

Personally I hate to see photos of fishermen holding their catch aloft, the bodies of fish hardened like plaster bats. Neither I, nor the numerous other fly fishermen of similar sentiment, are bleeding hearts who ruefully object to the primitive aspects of the sport. (I occasionally kill fish without suffering tormented and sleepless nights searching my soul.) But I am concerned with guaranteeing my offspring a heritage of "living" water and the creatures which put the "wild" in wilderness.

The continuation of the sport is contingent upon success tempered by benevolence and self-denial. To take as many fish as the law allows is extravagant and destructive. Fish limits today are too high, and fisheries maintenance is too low. Only the insecure sportsman needs an accumulation of wilted trout bodies to reassure his ego that he has won some kind of vague competition with nature.

The true fisherman is content with his proximity to water and the pursuit itself. To keep a brace of native trout is an occasional indulgence. To keep a limit of hatchery trout is merely a business proposition with the state—certainly such an endeavor is far removed from fishing. It is far better to return the vast majority of fish, domestic as well as wild, in the hope that they will breed superior and more vigorous generations.

The Fly Fisherman Activist

It is myopic and irresponsible to continually exploit the natural environment without reinvesting at least modest sums of time, energy, or even the vulgar medium of money. The future of fishing, the preservation of wild species, and the everlasting battle for quality water requires the efforts and attentions of all serious fly fishermen. Just buying a fishing license is not enough; a fishing license is merely a fractional mandate to the state to operate a marginal business of trout production, an agricultural enterprise which guarantees a relatively seasonal flow of trout raised like chickens, replete with caged spirits, and flesh that betrays the domestic aura in its oatmeal flavor.

The compelling battle that fly fishermen and all other sportsmen face is to reintroduce the word "quality" and all that it infers into the language of the law, the economy, the society and ultimately the environment. The challenge to the individual sportsman and concerned citizen is awesome, if not downright intimidating. But there is virtually no excuse for passivity. Fly fishing, by its very nature, is not a sedentary preoccupation, nor should it be pursued by apathetic subscribers. Active involvement is every fly fisherman's obligation.

"What can I do?" "I am only one." "A voice in the wilderness." Etc. There are a million rationalizations available to the non-participant. Imperatives do not change in the face of infinite excuses. While there are many who will disagree with me about how to precipitate change, I offer, nevertheless, several avenues to explore.

Learn to measure success in terms of experience, not in numbers of fish caught and cleaned. Use barbless hooks and return fish without damaging them. The fisherman must learn to handle fish confidently, decisively, and gently.

Despite the most sportsmanlike intentions of fishermen, many fish which are released will die anyway. This pointless mortality could be averted by proper handling. There is definitely a right way and a wrong way to liberate fish.

The first rule is not to overplay a fish. Exert the necessary pressure to subdue a hooked fish in the shortest time. Exhausting the animal causes lactic acid to accumulate in the blood stream. Assist a tired fish to recover by gently holding the animal upright in calm water. Its respiration can be stimulated by swaying it from side to side. When the fish can maintain its balance and its gills are pumping normally, then it can be released with a reasonable assurance of survival.

Do not manhandle, constrict or remove a fish from the water unless absolutely necessary. If possible, it is always best to twist the hook free from a fish while it is still in the water. Surgeon's forceps are especially useful for this delicate maneuver. A barbless hook is also an obvious aid in this endeavor. Incidentally, barbless hooks do not result in lost fish; improper playing does. If the hook, barbless or not, is imbedded too deeply in a sensitive area, do not attempt to remove it. Simply clip the line near the hook. The fish will dislodge the offending ornament with ease in an amazingly short time.

If it is necessary to handle the fish, do so with wet hands. Rough, dry hands are abrasive and will scrape away the mucous film which protects the fish from surface infections and fungus. Remember that a fish removed from water is literally drowning in space. Handle it quickly, confidently and gently.

Never touch the fish's gills as these are actually external lungs, which are as sensitive as the internal lungs of mammals. Even so-called experts on national television shows are often displayed conveniently raking a fish out of the water by its gill slits. Such indiscreet handling often results in fatal injuries.

Do not release a fish which is bleeding. A small drop of blood near the wound is normal, but any flow should signal the fisherman to quickly and humanely dispatch his catch.

The Northwest Indians believed that a man must accept the responsibility for the soul of any animal he killed. The conscientious fisherman should strongly consider such beliefs.

Whether catching fish or not, in weather fair or foul, the true outdoorsman will experience pleasure and reward in his sport. The fish are a bonus. Returning them is a gesture of enlightenment.

Become a political animal. Never mind the negative context of this statement. One of the best ways to fight dirty government is to procure "quality waters". The condition of the environment is far more than a metaphorical measure of the government.

Write to your Congressman and thank him when he introduces or supports bills that are ecologically sound. Express your disagreement and displeasure when your Congressman fails to protect the interests of the environment.

Join clubs, organizations and groups which are active in more than just social gatherings. Resign from organizations which fail to respond to the imperatives of ecological integrity. Provide financial support, however modest, for sound lobbying, for water rehabilitation and maintenance programs, and for lawsuits which are in the interest of quality waters.

Discount all bureaucratic pleas for sensible moderation. Too often the androids of government attempt to neutralize outrage and the emotive concerns of the informed and suspicious with carefully clouded and confusing rhetoric. The deceptions of governmental bureaucracies are almost without peer in the manipulative arts. When questioning policies, regulations, laws and programs, demand plain and simple language. Persist until all excess verbiage has been trimmed from the flanks of the issue at hand.

There is no substitute for well-directed anger. If people cannot generate anger as a reaction to the despoilation of the environment, then there is little left, indeed, hardly a purpose to the emotion at all.

I have a friend who is the proverbial gentleman and scholar. He is a reasonable and discriminating man. He is also the principal of a school in Washington State. Despite all of these solid character traits, the sight of a plane, or truck, or tractor with the symbol of the Army Corps of Engineers stenciled on the side will elicit from him the most obscene gestures and the most venom-flecked epithets to ever issue from a proper mouth. He is one among legions of Northwest fishermen who have suffered too much at the destructive forces of the engineering—conquer the earth—mentality.

Stay informed. Study all issues. Avoid the manufactured cliches. There is no substitute for knowledge. The success of the individual fly fisherman as well as the preservation of the species relies on reading, study, observation and a constant monitoring of every aspect of the sport. Intelligent reaction to change, good or bad, must be preceded by the skeptic's eye for detail.

No issue today can be regarded in isolation or as a separate entity. Fishermen must learn to generalize, to develop divergent as well as convergent styles of thinking. It is impossible to rationally consider the quality of any given water without also considering the riparian zone, the surrounding landscape, industry at large, land planning, logging, ranching, farming, recreation, and virtually every enterprise which remotely alters the environment. All habitats for fish and wildlife are contingent upon a total ecological vision.

Beware of unchallenged attitudes, ideas and policies. Many cliches remain dogma because few suspect that meaningless phrases are self perpetuating. There are so many such creatures of language that it is hard to know where to start, but I will single out the Departments of Fish and Wildlife in the Western States because of their ubiquitous, single mindedness of purpose.

Fishery departments are, almost without exception, slaves to quantity. Their definition of fine fishing is tied up in numbers. As long as the fisheries people continue to nurture this illusion, the public will continue to maintain the attitude that lots of wormy hatchery trout equals good sport. When challenged on the subject of a deteriorating fishery, the management people invariably respond with grandiose plans for rehabilitation, which includes the triple threat cliche: poison, plant and profit.

The first cliche involves the presence of coarse fish in a lake. Supposedly coarse fish compete with sport fish for the available resource, the assumption being that carp, minnows, suckers and a myriad of other fish will rob the water environs of the necessary food for trout. Where is the proof for this inflated claim? What statistical studies were used? Can this theory be generally applied to all waters? The curious thing is that most coarse fish live a different life style and consume a different diet than trout. Some coarse fish are primarily vegetarians. Almost all of these "enemies of the state" are a dietary supplement to trout, have always co-existed with sports fish, and are generally found where large trout are abundant.

The planting of uniform fish, all diminutive and equally anemic, is a seasonal answer to the opening day mania, but has little to do with the higher objectives of fishing. If a resource is depleted, the fisheries people rush to saturate the water with a plethora of witless creatures. Catch limits are rarely reduced despite the obvious need. Consequently, from season to season few trout survive and even fewer spawn. The fisheries people have ensured a cyclic phenomena of impotence.

On many of the quality lakes there is a regulation which prohibits the keeping of fish below 12 inches in length. Many of these lakes are the same ones appointed to periodic annihilation with poisons. The curious paradox exists in the fact that the larger trout are the most predacious. Those very fish which would control the populations of coarse fish are the same ones which fishermen are entitled to keep. Do the fisheries people prefer chemicals to a system of natural balance?

One of the most stubborn cliches embraced by the fisheries departments is the attitude that fly fishing is an elitist sport. Many fisheries people react so strongly to the presumed conspiracy inherent in fly only waters that there is little regard for the survival rates of fish. There is no statistical evidence which suggests that any method other than fly fishing with barbless hooks will hold mortality rates to below five percent.

Regulations are not administered as preferential treatment to humans but as preferential treatment to the fish. Examine other sports. Is it legal to hunt sitting geese with scopes on high-powered rifles? Should we be allowed to blast quail with cannon loads of grapeshot? What's wrong with netting ducks? Trapping deer? Digging clams with a steam shovel?

Every sport has to have built-in controls, modes of approach, and standards of behavior. The United States and Canada stand almost alone in their permissive attitudes toward the capture of game fish. In almost every other country blessed with major fresh-water fisheries, fly fishing is the norm. It is not regarded as a mystical craft reserved for the pompous upperclass nor as the esoteric medium of purists. From the very young to the old, fly fishing is the accepted form of the sport. In New Zealand there are only a few designated areas where gear other than the fly angling variety is even legal to use. In Australia, England, Scotland, Nova Scotia and parts of South America spin fishermen and bait fishermen are among the pitied minority. In other countries the people fly fish not only for the traditional rewards inherent in the art, but because it is in the nature of fly fishermen to discipline themselves, to control consumption, and to value the natural process of rejuvenation.

Not every country can afford the highly indulgent practice of restocking waters with furious abandon. Yet that is our style. Presumably a lake that does not give up a satisfactory quota of fish to each and every awkward angler is a bad risk. People will quit buying licenses. The government fish farms will suffer drought. The old supply and demand bugaboo will haunt administrators in their burial grounds of paper. In plain truth, the fisheries departments are paranoid about profits. Yet leisure activity is the number one industry in this country today, a sure thing.

Where is the evidence that more designated quality waters, a smaller catch limit, and modified regulations will result in a reduction of fishing enthusiasm? Too many people in authority have ignorantly maintained prejudices which are ultimately destructive. Too many bureaucrats feel that their jobs are somehow correlated to ice chests full of fish. There is a failure to recognize that the market philosophy does not extend to a healthy ecological domain. Balances must be struck by nature, not by waters stocked like shelves in a grocery store.

Chapter IX

Landing Without A Net:

A future Parable

e stood with his feet sinking into the muddy bank and his hands deeply buried in a cobalt blue coat. Drizzle purred through its own smoke. The onlooker watched the fisherman casting into the mist, an erect figure mitered to the lake shore, sawing at the air rhythmically.

The observer's question was formulated less out of curiosity than out of courtesy, a gesture of alliance in the rain. Yet the question was oddly analytical, awkwardly personal. "Why are you a fisherman?"

The fisherman allowed a short laugh, offered as an acknowledgment and perhaps a slight defense. It gave him time to make some sense out of an inner design he had never questioned.

The onlooker was in no hurry. He angled for answers with the same determination and remote sense of despair as the thoroughly evolved fisherman angled for his quarry. He watched the man cast and waited with certain patience. Fragments of the answer were inherent in the fisherman's grace and serene union with space. The fisherman's casting was a ballet fixed in time, grounded in flesh, negotiated in air, and finally grafted to water.

The fisherman worked effortlessly, playing at his proscribed task. The strangely ionized light, common to sun-shrouded mists, inscribed details with startling clarity. The fisherman's fibrous rod, a yellow, projecting tube of cartilage, emerged from the underside of his arm. A grommet of skin puckered, seeming to suck at the butt section of the high tensile, willow-like horn. Vascular lumps of muscle surrounded the projection. The highly-tempered rod was fused along the arm, but it diverged far enough back from the wrist to allow the fisherman's hand complete freedom of movement.

The line, a twisted, purple strand of tissue, issued from the web between his two central fingers, uncoiling from a reservoir somewhere inside his palm. At the end of the tapering braid of muscle was an internal complex of specialized silk glands. These highly developed glands generated and automatically replaced leader as fine and clear as plasticized mucous. A localized valve in the fisherman's cardio-vascular system determined whether the line would float or sink. The more oxygen dispersed into the micro-system of vessels and capillaries, the higher the line would float. The fisherman was in absolute control of his gear.

The fisherman retrieved his line, stripping it through the curled spurs of bone along the polished cartilage. Wet, glistening coils of line fell at his feet. He talked haltingly, offering a belated semblance of friendliness, as he removed the fly, clipping it precisely between two, flat, bevel-edged teeth.

"My father was a fisherman..." he laughed self consciously. "Obviously." He smiled and hooked the fly into a mat of thick hair on his scalp. "It's natural...a part of me, you might say."

The onlooker watched as the fisherman selected another fly and appraised the silver creation at length. The leader hung loosely down his arm as he held the rod aloft. The fisherman deliberated on the eye of the hook, a kinetic stare which commanded the line to undulate smoothly, seeking the eye of the hook like a hypnotized snake. The leader entered and performed the perfect contortions of a Palomar knot. The leader flexed, tightening to the exact micromatic test, a final binding. The onlooker recognized the nymph pattern. He approved silently. It was a Galactic Radiant, tied from the blended metallic fur of magnetized asteroid burrowers, on a No. 8 upeye, long shank, cold-forged zirconium hook...barbless, of course. The onlooker ventured an opinion with the hesitance of an ice walker.

"You can be whatever you want. Heritage is no obstacle. With a little genetic surgery..."

A wind blew across the water, a sudden thermal surge which seemed to intercept the words and sweep them backward up the bank.

The fisherman had caught enough corners of the statement to cube it in his mind and weigh its mass. But the wind persisted, providing an excuse to feign ignorance.

Before the onlooker could repackage his statement and hurl the parcel into the wind, a fish struck. The fisherman lifted his rod and stepped back; the excess line whirred swiftly into his palm. The onlooker realized that the fisherman had reacted several long, silent moments before the fish had flared into view, a semiphore of silver near the lake's surface. It was as if the hook had anticipated the fish.

The fisherman read the bramble of nerves in his line and leader. He knew the fish was firmly hooked in the corrugated mouth plate just below the nostrils. He could feel the leader scrape across the serrated jaw ridge as the fish skidded sideways.

During the battle neither man spoke. The fish leapt, touching tail to head, creating metallic, jolting U's in space. The water coughed up the fish and choked on its splashing descent several times.

The fisherman thought, "Perhaps this is the answer, this splicing of desperate action and reaction, the counterforces of capture and escape. It was a primitive concept."

The onlooker half stepped, half slid down the melting bank. Despite his questionable footing, his hands remained firmly entrenched in the long overcoat. He groped to a stop, assumed a posture of restraint and watched with continued detachment. It was a discipline nearly visible in his neck.

The fisherman seemed to anticipate the fish's every movement. He lowered and raised his rod, at one moment to compensate, at another moment to provoke. The line poured from the webbing between his fingers on runs, and the slack retracted as if consumed by an oiled vacuum when the fish relented. Water droplets glistened from the blue striations of tapered muscle. The cartilaginous rod was bent to a degree which seemed to defy all organic limits.

The struggle had somehow loosened his tongue. Perhaps the adrenalin had triggered a mechanism of clarity; thoughts that had been buried in purely physical association were suddenly flushed into the embarrassing light. He did not ease up on the fish as he talked.

"This preoccupation with water and the hydro-beasts...it releases me from myself. The throbbing of the snared animal, the context of struggle...it defuses all other concerns, short circuits mundane existence."

The fisherman began to dominate his captive. The rod flexed smoothly, sucking the fish toward the periphery of its universe. The thrashing of the fish was no longer extreme. Its final, desperate, defensive shudders sent muffled vibrations into the hollow of the fisherman's stomach...a primeval message.

The fisherman could feel the hook working free, a certain fine wallow in the line, a distant but accurate perception. The onlooker studied the large fish as it listed in the shallows. He knew it had not spent its last coin of will; a sudden incineration of blind energy was inevitable. He also sensed the hook sagging in the fish's flesh. The onlooker studied the fisherman's eyes from the side, searching the purple, bulbous lenses for a polarization of thought.

The fisherman interrupted the uneasy silence, slicing through the common fear of disappointment, of naked despondency rushing to fill the gap.

"Alone. That is the most basic element which makes me what I am—a fisherman. The isolation of the task, that is the sweet pulp of experience."

The onlooker understood, but he couldn't bear the threat of escape, the sudden cave-in of excitement. The line between exhilaration and exhaustion was finely drawn to the breaking point. He stepped closer to the water; he felt drawn to it. His right hand withdrew from the coat as if being unsheathed.

The large fish saw the two figures standing like dark totems on the water's horizon. Its every fiber echoed with the savage imperative of survival. The final flailing which would distinguish between life and death mounted in its dull interior.

The onlooker stepped into the lake, planting a pivot in the water. He leaned outward, crouching and extending, magnetized by the gleaming prize.

The fisherman leaned back, forcing a conclusion to the struggle. He felt the weight of the fish center between his shoulder blades.

The onlooker's wrist extended from the deep-blue tube of coat. It stretched from the sleeve, obscenely outward; the white skin was radiant with purpose. The fisherman offered distracted glances as the onlooker's hand began to unfold. The fingers spread like a spider awakening. As the two outer fingers uncurled in space, mutating growths, a net of knotted, filmy tendons unfurled and hung loosely below the distended hand.

The onlooker lowered his hand-net into the water, sliding it in at an oblique angle.

The massive fish wrenched violently, turning toward the deep. The fisherman responded, his wax-yellow rod bleached by pressure to tones of white where it curved radically. Without removing his eyes from the fish, he gently admonished the onlooker.

"I never use a net..."

INDEX

Anatomy of trout, 20
Aqua Bug, 41
Artificials—types, 25
Beetles, 40
Black and White, 32
Black Collar, 44
Bloom, 11
Brooks, Charles, 26
Caddisflies, 32
Carey Special, 46
Chopaka Lake, 54
Chrome Bug, 37
Crawfish, 35
Cream Caddis, 34
Damselflies, 42
Damselfly Nymph, 43
Davis Lake, 53
Doll's Hair, 48
Dragonflies, 44
Emergent Mosquito, 35
Epilimnion, 11
Fish Lake, 59
Fly lines, 17
Fly reels, 18
Fly rods, 16
Ghost Bug, 37
Giant Crawfish, 37
Giant Water Bug, 42
Golden Girl, 40
Greenhead, 31
Heather Nymph, 43
Higgins Reservoir, 60
Hypolimnion, 12
Jewel Lake, 59
Jindabyne Special, 48

Kaufmann, Randall, 25
Lake Chelan, 52
Lake Lenice, 62
Lakestone, 39
Leisenring Lift, 53
Little Green Caddis, 33
Mayflies, 30
Meniscus, 10
Mongrel, 47
Moose Mane, 33
Mosquitoes, 34
Nondescript, 47
Public Enemy No. 1, 35
Purple Phantom, 47
Releasing fish, 68
Rosborough, Polly, 46
Rosenbaum, Squeak, 46
Rosenbaum's Dragonfly Nymph, 47
Scuds, 35
Schwiebert, Ernest, 24
Seaweed's Crawdad, 38
Shrimp, 35
Sowbugs, 35
Stoneflies, 38
Thermocline, 11
Timberline, 31
Timberline Emerger, 31
Trueblood Shrimp, 36
Unity Reservoir, 38
Unkempt, 33
Warm Springs Reservoir, 64
Water Bugs, 40
West Medical Lake, 50
Yellowstone Lake, 56
Zug Bug, 41